ID0868974

One Hundred Years of

THE AMERICAN TWO-MOVE CHESS PROBLEM

by Kenneth S. Howard

A Collection of 212 Compositions
by United States Problemists

Second Edition

Dover Publications, Inc. New York

Published in Canada by General Publishing Company, Ltd., 30 Lesmill Road, Don Mills, Toronto, Ontario.
Published in the United Kingdom by Constable and Company, Ltd., 10 Orange Street, London WC 2.

The American Two-Move Chess Problem is a new work, first published by Dover Publications in 1962.

International Standard Book Number: 0-486-20997-0
Library of Congress Catalog Card Number: 63-2646

Manufactured in the United States of America.
Dover Publications, Inc.
180 Varick Street
New York, N. Y. 10014

Preface

AT VARIOUS TIMES chess problem lovers have suggested to the author the desirability of making and publishing a collection of "the best problems ever composed." That would be a large order indeed! Even if limited to problems by American composers, it would be a monumental task. So the author has chosen the more modest assignment of making a selection of *two-movers* by United States problemists that conform to standards of construction which he considers typical of the best American work.

As explained in the first chapter, the author believes that what may be regarded as the ideal American two-mover is an attractively set composition, illustrating an interesting strategic idea, introduced by a subtle keymove. This is the standard on which he has based his selections.

In the more recent developments of the American two-mover, there has, at times, been a tendency with some composers to slight the importance of good keymoves, possibly because of foreign influences. Yet unless problems offer some difficulty of solution they are likely to degenerate into mere illustrations of mechanisms, of possible interest to certain composers but with little appeal to the solver.

The average solver enjoys discovering a subtle or spectacular keymove, as Comins Mansfield so aptly states in his *Adventures in Composition*: "but let it [the key] be well hidden or let it contain some element of surprise or charm, and the solver will recall it with pleasure long after he has forgotten all the studied intricacies which the composer blended laboriously into his problem. Nine out of ten solvers are not classifiers of themes. They want the simple pleasure of solving, not the intellectual rapture of discovering a new relationship of the pieces in a difficult theme."

The problem art depends on the support of the solver, and the popularity and lasting "life" of any individual problem is determined by its appeal to the solving public. The compositions in this collection have been chosen for their all-around artistic excellence, and the author is confident that in the emphasis he has placed on the importance of good keymoves he will have the unqualified support of an overwhelming majority of solvers.

In assembling this collection the aim has been to show the finest two-movers of American origin irrespective of their composers. This is a different approach to that of *A Sketchbook of American Chess Problematists* (the third book in the Frank Altschul series), which was designed to give some examples of the work of all the better known American composers. The present collection, however, has compositions by fifty-eight problemists, and so actually includes representative work of the leading figures in the American two-move field.

In making his selections the author has had the cooperation of most of the more prominent living United States composers, who have sent him what they regard as their best compositions, from which he has picked the positions that in his judgment meet the standards set for the collection.

Since starting work on the collection several years ago, five of the major collaborators have died: Alain White, who gave enthusiastic encouragement and made many constructive suggestions; Otto Wurzburg and Geoffrey Mott-Smith, who furnished selections of problems by many composers published in problem departments they had edited and from other sources; Dr. E. P. Keeney, who supplied copies of many positions from the files of the *Cincinnati Enquirer*, in which for many years he conducted an outstanding problem department; and Edgar W. Allen, who furnished copies of problems from various sources and spent long hours in looking up or verifying sources and dates of publication.

The author also is indebted to Edgar Holladay, Nicholas Gabor and Eric M. Hassberg for similar cooperation.

From the wealth of material thus made available practical publication limitations have made it necessary to restrict the selections to two hundred twelve positions.

The initial version of the manuscript was read by Alain White, but the responsibility for the selections is entirely the author's, except that Mr. White suggested which of the author's own compositions to include.

K. S. H.

East Orange, New Jersey
February, 1962

Note to Second Edition

SEVERAL typographical errors, both in the text and in the diagrams, have been corrected in this edition.

Sheppard's No. 160 has been replaced with another of his compositions that is more noteworthy.

Wurzburg's No. 132 was found to have been anticipated by a problem by Godfrey Heathcote that was reproduced on page lxxviii of *Chess Lyrics*. Accordingly another of Wurzburg's compositions has been substituted for it.

Then it has been called to the attention of the author that his problem on page 91 (published in 1936) was anticipated by one by Sándor Hertmann, published in 1925. The positions are identical, except for the location of the white king, which is immaterial, since he takes no part in the play.

November, 1964   K.S.H.

Contents

The American Heritage

TRADITIONALLY the American chess problem dates from Loyd. As Paul Morphy eclipsed all previous American chess players, so Sam Loyd, born in 1841, four years after Morphy, so far outshone earlier American problem composers that he is commonly looked upon as the father of the American chess problem.

Loyd was preeminently a three-move composer and actually did not compose any great number of two-move problems. Yet his influence on American composition was so marked that characteristics of his style are seen throughout the work of a large proportion of American problemists and have affected American two-move composition to a definite degree.

The major portion of Loyd's problem work was done before he was twenty-one, but his banner was ably carried on by Shinkman, "The Wizard of Grand Rapids." Six years younger than Loyd, William A. Shinkman did not begin to compose until about 1870. Then, for some sixty years, he turned out such a steady volume of problems as to become the most prolific of American composers. Interested in problems of all types, Shinkman did magnificent work in multi-move compositions. Although his two-move output was limited in comparison with the number of his longer problems, many of his two-movers are sparkling gems. With ideals similar to those of Loyd, Shinkman should be credited with playing an influential part in moulding the course of the American two-mover.

A third outstanding early problemist, who had much in common with Loyd and Shinkman, was William Meredith. From the Good Companion days his name has been given to two-movers where the total men employed do not exceed twelve. Meredith, however, restricted his contributions to a

1

few publications and probably had little influence on contemporary composition. There was no wide recognition of his talent until after his death.

The ideal problem, characteristic of all three of these composers, had a sharply expressed idea, introduced by a subtle key, set in a light and attractive manner. Although only an occasional problem attained this perfection, it was the goal toward which these problemists aimed.

The ideals of Loyd and Shinkman have had a permanent influence on American problem composition, and while they themselves were most successful in applying such ideals to three-move and longer problems, their standards of composition unquestionably were reflected in the two-move field. In fact, their ideals have persisted to the present day in the composition of the better two-move problems of a sufficient proportion of outstanding American problemists, so that they may be considered as typical of the most artistic American two-move work.

It may be noted parenthetically, that in some European countries various leading composers have focused their interest almost exclusively on thematic mechanisms. Sometimes such problemists seem willing to utilize almost any key, even if colorless, that assures a sound position, then there are other composers who apparently pay little regard to attractiveness of setting.

Of the outstanding characteristics of his ideal problem, Loyd placed first attractiveness of setting, or as he termed it, "neatness of position." He remarked in his *Strategy*, "I will remind our problemists once again that they are composing for the general public and not for the few experts who are able to solve a problem involving many moves or many pieces. I again refer to neatness of position as being the most important feature that constitutes a pleasing and popular problem."

Today, problem authorities would probably rate piquancy of idea or thematic novelty as the most important element, but to attract the attention of the solver in the first place, an inviting appearance is essential.

A lightly set problem is not necessarily an economically constructed one, and conversely a heavyweight composition may be built most economically. Economy of construction, as understood by problemists, means that the men used, especially the white pieces, are, as far as possible, each employed in two or more capacities and that no more powerful men are used than are required for the specific purpose. For example, a queen should not function merely as a rook or bishop.

Naturally it is easier to attain a high degree of economy in a three-move or four-move problem than in a two-mover, because the additional moves give the composer a much greater opportunity to make more than one, or perhaps several, uses of each of the more powerful men in his composition.

Yet even though there is not so much scope for constructional economy in a two-mover, it is a quality that is appreciated by the discerning solver, who is pleased when he sees how a composer has shown his skill by making a man perform several functions, each in perhaps a different variation. Despite this distinction between lightness of setting and true economy, they also have a close relationship, since a composer may be able to achieve a light setting through his ability to secure maximum economy in his use of materials.

From the early days of the American chess problem, economy of construction has tended to supersede mere lightness of setting as a criterion of good workmanship; especially from the Good Companion days, because the complexity of many modern themes precludes light settings. Furthermore, interesting themes, which are possible of expression in light settings, have been rather thoroughly worked out, so that when a composer constructs a good lightweight two-mover today, there is a great likelihood he will find it has been anticipated.

On the other hand, in those rare instances where a problemist is so fortunate as to find an original idea that he can render in a light setting, he can count on the problem having a far wider appeal to solvers than many a heavier weight composition of equal thematic originality. Striking examples of this are such miniatures as Mott-Smith's No. 136, Neuhaus' No. 142 and Hassberg's No. 179 in this collection.

A generation ago much stress was laid on the various schools of problem composition. Even in 1921, H. Weenink in *Het Schaakprobleem: Ideën en Scholen*, translated into English and reprinted as the 1926 volume of Alain White's *Christmas Series*, devoted the first half of his treatise to an historical sketch of the more prominent schools. That today little attention is paid to any possible difference between schools of composition is largely due to two developments: the increasing internationalism of problem composition and the dominance of the two-mover over other lengths of problems.

The two-mover does not permit of nearly so much variety in manner of treatment as do longer problems and consequently affords less opportunities for composers to develop marked distinctions in their style of composition. Of course this is not a hard-and-fast rule, as witness the contrast between some of the lightweight gems that Mott-Smith was so adept in producing and many of the luxuriant compositions in which Fink reveled. These, however, are extremes.

Fashions in subject matter, which have varied from decade to decade, have in themselves had considerable influence on the style of the American two-mover. Yet many American problemists, whether constructing complete block positions, attempting extreme tasks or illustrating highly technical mechanisms have endeavored, often most successfully, to make their compositions meet the artistic standard that requires an attractive setting, good key and economical construction.

In the earlier period of American composition that ran roughly to the beginning of the present century, it was not especially difficult to attain such a standard, since whatever strategic play was made the content of a problem was usually shown in a comparatively simple form. But when the cult of the task problem began to become dominant, and as the tasks illustrated became more extreme, it was found to be increasingly difficult to observe artistic standards. Sometimes any kind of key was tolerated that would yield a sound position, economical renderings became rarities and attractiveness of setting was often disregarded. That it was not always impossible, however, to achieve impeccable task settings is shown by such positions as Nos. 28, 30 and 70.

The next notable period for the two-mover was that which arose through the activities of the Good Companion Chess Problem Club, which became international in its membership. This organization was not only founded by James F. Magee, Jr., of Philadelphia, but owed its years of successful progress in a large measure to his continued interest and administrative ability. In the Good Companion period composers began to combine, or blend, the more simple strategic ideas into elaborate structures, which in some cases became fantastically complex, and it was during these times that the term "theme complex" was coined.

An event of this period, which has had far-reaching influence, was the recognition—one could almost call it the discovery—of the half-pin. Although a few examples of the half-pin had appeared in problems of a far earlier date—a half-pin was used in a problem by W. Greenwood published in 1859—its thematic interest and constructional possibilities were not really appreciated until 1915, when the term "half-pin" originated in correspondence between Comins Mansfield, the English two-move genius, and the American composer, Murray Marble.

Many of the Good Companion problems ran to such complex extremes that attractive settings and good keys were rarely obtainable except by a stroke of luck. Yet a few, even of the more elaborate positions, conformed to artistic standards.

Besides such complex compositions, commonly associated with the Good Companion name, the Club also fostered the composing of lightweight problems which, while perhaps not attracting so much attention at the time, resulted in the production of many positions that will be remembered and enjoyed by solvers long after more ambitious and complicated contemporary work is forgotten. Problems with a total of twelve men or less were termed "Merediths," in honor of William Meredith (1835–1903), the Philadelphian composer, and numerous tourneys for Merediths, sponsored by the Club, led to the production of many delightful positions, such as Nos. 46, 47, 57, 61, 62, 71 and 77.

Another type which received considerable attention from a few American composers of that period was the complete block, or waiting-move problem, especially where some of the mating moves apparently set in the initial position were changed by the key, for which Brian Harley, the English problem authority, coined the apt name *mutate*. Several problemists did brilliant work in this field; and Charles Promislo specialized in such problems with outstanding success.

For a dozen years after the Good Companion days the tendency was toward the composition of problems with less extreme effects than characterized much of the later Good Companion work, and with greater emphasis on artistic settings. The restrained style of Comins Mansfield undoubtedly had much influence on American composition at this time.   It was during these years that the larger proportion of the author's own two-move work was published.

In the early thirties the brilliant technician, Alexander Kish, began producing two-movers which, although not exhibiting any marked novelty of ideas, were notable for the artistry with which the composer treated familiar themes.

During the later thirties a change in the character of the two-mover came about through differences in general thematic content.   Greater attention began to be given to the play of the white forces, instead of placing the emphasis on the interplay of the black men.   Line openings and closings, particularly as they affect the white pieces, were studied intensively, as were also dual avoidance and the operation of contingent threats.

Then with the publication in 1943 of *Variation Play* by Walter Jacobs and Alain White, the sixth book in Frank Altschul's beautiful chess problem series, an entirely new vista was opened in the possibilities of black mechanisms, in which great interest has since been taken, especially in the exploration of third-degree play.

It would be misleading, however, to attempt to partition off into definite periods with any great exactitude the progress of American two-move composition, stating that each period was characterized by some special type of problem.   While particular types flourished, and perhaps were even dominant, in certain years, many fine two-movers of other types were composed and published during those same years.

One reason for this is that the composing life of many eminent American problemists has extended over several different periods, and some composers have had individualized styles which have been but little affected by temporary trends in the fashions of composition.   For example, Shinkman, who began to compose in the early eighteen-seventies, and Dr. Bettmann, who began ten years later, were both active during and after the Good Companion days.   Yet neither indulged in the extreme complexities that characterized so much of the work of the latter part of that period.

Many other American composers have styles that are definitely individualistic. Fink delighted in positions with many pieces, yet his problems are inviting in appearance and he laid particular stress on excellence of keymoves. In Eaton's most typical work there is a liberal use of men and considerable complexity. On the other hand Shinkman's finest two-movers were lightweights, and most of Wurzburg's gems were exceedingly light in construction. Mott-Smith composed many good problems with numerous men, but he is best known in the two-move field for his remarkable skill in lightweight composition. From Dr. Dobbs' prolific output, he probably will be remembered the longest for some of his dainty lightweights.

Among American composers, in addition to Wurzburg, who have laid especial stress on elegance of presentation, Gamage, Sheppard and Jacobs have been outstanding for their consummate artistry. These problemists often have worked on-and-off for months on some position in the endeavor to secure the *ultimate* setting, and Gamage once stated that he was only interested in themes which he could show in an artistic dress.

From the study of the best two-move work of American problemists, extending throughout the past century, the author believes he is justified in believing that the great body of such compositions have sufficient common characteristics to support the contention that there is a typical American style of two-move composition.

Although signal exceptions to such a generalization may easily be pointed out, and despite temporary changes in fashions of composition, it may well be claimed that the typical American two-mover exhibits in an inviting and economical setting, a clean-cut strategic idea, introduced by an excellent keymove.

This combination of features is the criterion the author has used in selecting the following collection of problems, and most of the compositions chosen will be found to meet these high standards. Task problems and illustrations of interesting mechanisms, however successfully the composer may have achieved his immediate objective, are not included unless they also meet artistic standards of composition.

An example of what may be regarded as a borderline case is the inclusion of Dr. Bettmann's No. 79 which has an unprovided flight-capture in the initial setting and a fairly apparent key-move. The economy and attractiveness of the position, however, is so remarkable that the author does not believe anyone will feel that this masterpiece should have been omitted.

Types of Problems

BECAUSE of the chronological arrangement of the problems in this collection, compositions related by type of construction or by theme may be widely separated. In examining the collection, however, the reader may wish to compare problems of similar genre. To make it easier for him to do this, the author, in the present chapter and the two succeeding ones, in commenting on various problemistic characteristics and themes, refers to problems in which such features are exemplified.

In the earlier period of American composition many problems were composed expressly to show a striking or subtle keymove, Brock's No. 24 being an excellent example. Without its astonishing key No. 24 would be a rather flat affair. From Loyd's day even to present times, however, occasional fine positions have been published where the key is the motif of the composition—such as Wurzburg's No. 53 and No. 133. Gamage's No. 148 is built around its pleasing withdrawal keymove.

Although No. 172 has other points of interest, the sparkle comes largely from the odd, flight-giving key; while Nos. 74, 114 and 156 owe much of their charm to the surprise of the solver when he finds that the key is a king move.

The key of No. 11 is quietly subtle rather than spectacular, and that of No. 56 changes a set mate in an unusual way. No. 85 was composed specifically for the key, as also was No. 137. Many other problems in the collection have exceedingly fine keys, introducing thematic or otherwise interesting afterplay.

Akin to problems primarily composed for their keys are those constructed specifically for some tempting try. Sometimes a good try can be introduced as an embellishment after a problem is otherwise completed, or it may come through a lucky break in the course of construction. In some instances, how-ever, the try is the essence of the problem. Such is the case with No. 31, which Jokisch composed expressly to deceive the experienced but hasty solver. The author used the same idea in No. 105. In each of these problems the try is defeated by only a single, rather obscure defense.

In Fink's No. 38, the enticing try 1 Pc4, met only by 1 — — Pf6, was probably the basic idea of the problem. 1 Pc4 opens a line for the queen to mate by 2 Qd2, defeated by 1 — — P × Pep, which, however, permits 2 Q × B mate; so natural appearing a line of play that the solver may be loath to pass it up.

A type of composition, less common today than formerly, is where the interest centers in a brilliant mainplay and the secondary variations are merely incidental. The Bettmann brothers' No. 7 is an early example. Later excellent illustra-tions are Cooke's No. 88; and Winings' No. 113, with the quaint effect that results from the transfer of the white knights from their positions on the fifth rank to corresponding ones on the third. The setting is actually an example of a white half-pin. The point of Windle's No. 61 is the piquant mainplay, 1 Pc4, Qd6; 2 Pc5.

While in many problems the threat mate is colorless, or downright "brutal," occasionally it is the highlight of the composition. Holladay's No. 169 has various attractive features, but it is the odd threat, the withdrawal of the white knight to rook's eighth, that gives the problem its distinct individuality.

Two-movers illustrative of modern themes usually are threat problems, but all the various forms of waiting-move problems are richly represented in the gallery of American problem composition.

In earlier days incomplete blocks were more common than now, and Nos. 18 and 19 are typical examples, with striking keys. In each a mate is provided in the initial position for all but one black move. A particularly beautiful recent specimen is Gamage's No. 141, which may prove difficult to solve because the solver may be led to expect a threat problem from the open setting.

Excellent complete blocks by American composers are so numerous that attention will be called only to some outstanding examples. Eaton's elegant No. 140 illustrates what is termed a "vanishing dual." In the initial position, if black moves either knight to e2 there are mates by either white rook, but after the key only the queen's rook can mate. The apparent dual has vanished. There also is an added mate, 1 — — Pe3; 2 Sd7.

A famous complete block, with added mates, is Meredith's No. 10, with its spectacular key. In the oddly set No. 142 black is in a stalemate position, but the withdrawal key gives him four options, each followed by a different mate. Perhaps a distinct designation should be given to this type of problem.

Fink's No. 72 illustrates, in lightweight setting, what is termed a pendulum change. The keymove transposes two of the mates without changing their form. If black plays Qb4, before the key white can mate by Rb5 × Q; after the key the mate is Rb3 × Q. Before the key 1 — — Q × Rb3 is a self-block; after the key 1 — — Q × Rb5 is a self-block.

This type of problem might be considered as a transition form between the simple complete block and the complete block with changed play, the mutate. The collection has many fine examples of the latter, from Shinkman's day to the present time.

More than any other type of problem, the attractiveness of a mutate is dependent on the excellence of its construction. Not only should it show some piquant changes between the apparent and the actual mates, but the setting should be open and inviting in appearance. No. 6 is typical of Shinkman's style. The Bettmann brothers' No. 8 is rather heavily set, but it has a smart key and two of the set mates are replaced by more attractive ones. The third change, that after 1 — — Ke4, illustrates the vanishing dual.

Holladay's Meredith No. 157 is a peculiarly interesting type of mutate. In the initial position any move of the black queen is met by 2 Qd3, but after the keymove each of the three black queen moves requires a different mate.

Charles Promislo during Good Companion days was especially interested in complete blocks, and Nos. 41, 45, 50, 63 and 77 are brilliant illustrations of his remarkable skill in constructing mutates.   In No. 41 two mates are changed and three new mates added; in No. 45 four mates are changed and two are added; in No. 50 there are practically four changed and two added mates; in No. 63 three mates are changed and one added.   His marvelous No. 77 shows a complete change of half-pin mates in a classic setting.

Wurzburg's No. 116 is a particularly fine example of a mutate whose character is not immediately suggested by its setting.   It takes some inspection for the solver to recognize that the position is a complete block, since at first glance the locations of the white king and queen do not appear to be fixed.

No. 115 is of special interest because Kish made only a few experiments with this type of problem, most of his work illustrating sharply defined strategic themes, usually with threat keys.   Dobbs' No. 139 probably was not rated higher in the tourney award because of the duals after indifferent moves of the black queen.

The mutate reaches the acme of interest when it is made the medium for some thematic study.   No. 70 is a famous example. It is primarily a task problem with eight self-blocking moves. The wonderful key, 1 Rc8, changes the mate after 1 — — S × P from 2 KR × P to 2 Sc7.

Many problems have been constructed to show three discovered mates from a diagonal pawn battery, with a fourth mate given directly by the pawn, but the mutate setting gives an individual flavor to No. 127.

In the initial position of Beers' No. 130 there are two pin-mates following moves of the black king.   The key yields a third flight, with a third pin-mate.   These multiple pin-mates may be regarded as constituting the theme of the problem.

Wurzburg in No. 133 utilizes a mutate setting to show a charming illustration of a Bristol withdrawal key.   This may be considered as a pure withdrawal move, for although the rook is used for the mate after 1 — — R × Q, that mate is already set and the white rook's retreat to a8 is made solely to effect a clearance for the queen.

No. 81 is a particularly interesting example of the use of a mutate setting, inasmuch as the problem was composed to illustrate a complex theme: a line-pinned white piece moves along the line of pin and unpins a black unit by interference on another white piece, and then the unpinned black man, in its turn, unpins the key-piece allowing it to mate, viz., 1 Rf4, Pe4; 2 R × Pf5. No. 81 was one of the pioneer examples of the Howard theme and its setting in mutate form was due to the constructive skill of Alain White.

The block-threat came into notice about 1905, and was studied most intensively in the half-dozen years from 1910 to 1915. Since then occasional fine examples have been composed from time to time.

Shinkman's skill in the composition of this type of problem is shown in Nos. 33 and 34. An especially pleasing specimen, because of its light weight, open setting, good key and complete change of mates, is No. 48 by Rice. One of the most famous block-threats ever composed is Dr. Bettmann's No. 73, with its splendid key and unexpected threat. Other excellent examples are Nos. 64, 69 and 76.

The introduction of changed-mate play in threat problems offers wide possibilities. When from the general appearance of a position the solver recognizes it as a threat problem, he ordinarily will not be expecting changed-mate play as he would from a block setting, and this may add considerably to the difficulty and pleasure in discovering the solution. Then the threat problem does not impose on the composer such constructive restrictions as does the complete block, since mates do not have to be provided in the initial setting for every possible black move. This frequently enables the problemist to secure a more open and attractive setting than he could in a block position. It also may permit him to utilize some natural appearing black defensive move as a basis for a set line of play that is changed in the actual solution.

Sometimes only a single, conspicuous line of play may be changed; in other cases there may be two or more changed mates. The changes in Nos. 149 and 183 are the thematic essence of the problems. In No. 149 four different mates by white's king's knight's pawn are set to meet moves of the black queen, viz., 1 — — Qf3; 2 P × Q: 1 — — Qh3; 2 P × Q: 1 — — Q × S; 2 Pg3: 1 — — Qg5; 2 Pg4. After the key, 1 Qb1, it is the queen's bishop's pawn that delivers four mates to meet defensive moves of the black queen.

John F. Barry's No. 59 is a hybrid type. At first glance the position may appear to be a block because mates are set for so many black moves, but further inspection will show that no mates are provided for 1 — — Bb4 and 1 — — Bc7. Actually the problem is solved by a threat key, but it is not a true block-threat since the initial position is not a complete block. The point of the problem is that the solver may be loath to abandon the set line, 1 — — Q × B ck; 2 Q × Q. The dual after 1 — — Qf6 ck is a fly in the amber, as mate can be given either by 2 B × Q or by the cross-check, 2 Bg6.

In Mott-Smith's exquisite miniature, No. 94, one return capture mate is replaced by another that is a model mate. The capture of the queen, 1 — — R × Q, is also followed by a model mate.

No. 97 is an elaborate affair in which two set mates by 2 K × Q are replaced by return capture mates by the white knights. The king–queen battery is so familiar a device, and is set so suggestively, that the solver may hesitate some time before disregarding it.

The mechanisms of Dr. Dobbs' Nos. 47 and 62 are more simple. In the initial positions of each of these problems there is a conspicuous self-pinning capture check by the black queen, where white can mate by a return capture. In each instance white gives up the set mate and threatens a mate that will be unaffected by black's checking capture, but which will be a cross-check if black makes the capture. The beauty of these positions lies in the subtlety of the keys and the daintiness of the settings.

In No. 98 two set mates in the initial position are changed by the key. As set, if 1 — — K × KP, white can mate by 2 Pd4; and if 1 — — P × S, by 2 QP × P. Both these mates are changed by the key, 1 Qg1, viz., 1 — — K × KP; 2 Pf4, and 1 — — P × S; 2 Pf3, this latter variation illustrating the Schiffmann Defense.

A further embellishment, of major interest, is that there is a try, 1 Qe1, defeated only by 1 — — Qc8, which is followed by still another change in these two lines: 1 Qe1, K × KP; 2 Q × P, and 1 — — P × S: 2 Qe3, introducing mates that differ both from the initially set mates and from those in the actual solution. This feature apparently did not attract attention when the problem was published, but in more recent years composers have shown considerable interest in such virtual changed mates in tries, that do not occur in the actual solution.

A modern thematic adaptation of changed-mate play in a threat problem is presented in Buchwald's No. 183. As set a random move of the black knight leads to mate by 2 Qd2, and the correction move, 1 — — Se4, is met by 2 Qd3. A second correction line is 1 — — S × P; 2 S × S. After the key, however, a random move of the knight, defeating the threat of 2 Q × P, permits mate by the contingent threat 2 Rh3. Again 1 — — Se4 is a correction, but now it is met by 2 Sg4. 1 — — Sf5 is another correction, which allows mate by 2 Qe5.

Although numerous beautiful miniatures—problems with a total of seven or less men—have been composed in three-move and four-move lengths, it is extremely difficult to construct a two-move miniature that has much thematic interest. Besides this, so many two-move miniatures have been published in past years that today few experienced problemists attempt to work in so light a medium, because there is so great a likelihood they will find their efforts anticipated.

Mott-Smith, however, achieved notably original results in this specialized field, as witness his Nos. 94, 122 and 136.

A pleasing feature in many problems is the apparent freedom of movement of certain black pieces, especially that of the black queen, which provides the chief defenses in Nos. 15, 55 and 170, and plays a conspicuous role in Nos. 47 and 62. In No. 136 she is the sole black man beside the king. She is freed by the key to take the limelight in Nos. 34, 61, 73 and 151, all of which are exceptionally interesting compositions.

The task problem, which develops the maximum possibilities in illustrating some thematic element, has had a strong appeal to American composers. The cult of the task was pursued most assiduously during the first two decades of the century; first in a study of more simple forms, and later, in the Good Companion days, in more complex compositions.

Nos. 23 and 52 show three diagonally discovered checks from the moves of a black pawn. In No. 27 the king makes the keymove and then discovers mate in two variations, laterally and diagonally, doubling the Durbar theme.

Nos. 28 and 29 are examples of the task known as the Queen's Cross, in which the white queen delivers mate from twelve different squares, again a maximum. The various possible modes of the Queen's Cross were studied by J. C. J. Wainwright, Walter I. Kennard, Frederick Gamage and other contemporary composers, and Wainwright wrote an essay on the subject illustrated with fifty-two examples. This was included in *Les Tours de Force sur l'Echiquier*, the 1906 volume of Alain White's *Christmas Series*.

As explained on page 67 of *The Good Companion Two-Mover*, Wainwright "showed that the total positions which the Queen could occupy on the chessboard in all the problems exemplifying the task formed a cross of twenty squares: b5 - d5 - d7 - e7 - e5 - g5 - g4 - e4 - e2 - d2 - d4 - b4 - b5, the mating Queen always standing on one of the squares within the cross, while the checked King occupied another."

Marble's No. 30 shows six self-blocks on the same square following the capture of a white piece. Although other composers have illustrated this task, none has surpassed the elegance of Marble's version. An attractive rendering by Sheppard, No. 200, has five self-blocks on the same square. The wonderful No. 70, with its eight self-blocks on various squares, has already been mentioned.

In Fink's No. 67 two black pawns each make two interferences on a single black rook. In Sheppard's No. 71 a pawn promotes to a knight on three different squares, while in Dr. Bettmann's marvelous No. 79 a pawn promotes to a knight or queen on three different squares, the six promotions being differentiated by black's play.

Beers' No. 103 is an example of a complete Black Knight Wheel, each of the eight moves of the black knight forcing a different mating move. In No. 96, by ingenious constructive technique, Fink achieves the difficult task of showing mutual interferences between the black queen and the two black bishops.

Strategic Elements

WHILE several strategic elements frequently are combined in a two-move problem, in many compositions one element is outstanding. A composer often constructs a position specifically to illustrate, for example, black interferences, cross-checks, some of the various types of pinning and unpinning, or pawn promotions. There are numerous problems in the collection in which one of such strategic elements is distinctly the dominant feature, and many of these will be noted briefly in this chapter.

The collection is rich in examples of the different forms of interference between black men; both where such interference is the motif of the composition and where it is only incidental to some other feature. Black interference is of particular interest where it is mutual between two black men and leads to two distinct mates.

In Holladay's No. 181 there is a mutual Grimshaw interference—between rook and bishop—on b5, and in addition there is a related interference by the bishop on the other rook when black plays 1 — — Bc2. Nos. 1, 21, 35, 158, 166 and 175 show doubled mutual Grimshaws. In No. 166 there is also an interference by the knight on the black queen's rook. Nos. 1 and 21 have what has been dubbed the "Organ Pipes" arrangement of the black interfering pieces.

Fink's No. 66 shows what T. R. Dawson, in the April, 1940, issue of the *British Chess Magazine*, termed "unit Grimshaws," in which a rook and bishop interfere with each other on different squares, instead of interfering on the same square as in the previous examples. In No. 66 the bishop interferes with the rook on b5, while the rook interferes with the bishop on d5. There is also a pawn-Grimshaw interference on e6, and 1 — — Pe5 is an interference on the rook.

Pawn-Grimshaws are doubled in Rice's No. 40.   A Nowotny interference is the leading feature of Meredith's No. 9.   Two interferences of a pawn on a rook appear in DeBlasio's No. 187. Two interferences by each of two pawns on a single rook are shown in Fink's No. 67, as has previously been mentioned.   A pawn interferes with two rooks in turn in No. 99.

No. 36, a famous problem, has two interferences by a pawn on the black queen, and this form of interference is called the Gamage theme because of this problem.   In mating white can safely unpin the black queen following each interference. This type of play is sometimes also known as the Przepiorka theme, after the Polish composer D. Przepiorka, especially where the black piece unpinned in the mate is a rook instead of the queen.

In No. 14 a rook interferes on the two bishops.   In No. 32 there is the same relationship in the setting of the rook and the bishops, but here it is the bishops that interfere on the rook. A bishop interferes on a rook twice in No. 107.   The mutual interference between a queen and two bishops is shown in No. 96; and that between a queen and rook in No. 104.

Each of the two black knights in Fink's No. 75 interferes in turn on the queen and on the queen's bishop, making four thematic interferences in all.   The half-pinning of the knights adds pleasingly to the complexity of the composition.   In No. 63 the knights also interfere on the queen.

The collection has several attractive examples of black interferences that are more or less incidental to the motif of the composition.   In Nos. 124, 144 and 154 there are mutual Grimshaw interferences which are secondary in thematic interest to other features of the problems.

Vinje's No. 124 primarily illustrates unpinning of two white pieces by the withdrawal of the black pinning pieces, the rook and bishop that make the mutual Grimshaw interference. Gamage's No. 144 is a complex composition in which a Grimshaw on c4, and an interference of bishop on rook on d7, are combined with other pleasing play.   Two bishops interfere with a rook in No. 108 to bring about the two thematic mates in what the author has christened "pawn-one-two play."

In the problems just considered a black man interferes with the guarding or attacking power of some long-range black piece

—queen, rook or bishop. Where it is a white man that interferes with a black line of influence, the interference is commonly termed a shut-off. It is this type that occurs in a cross-check, where a white man shuts off a check to the white king and simultaneously gives mate—in a two-mover—either by a direct or a discovered check. The only form of cross-check in which such a shut-off is not utilized is where the white king himself moves out of range of a black check and at the same time discovers check.

In early days it was regarded as a feat to permit black to give double-check in a two-mover, particularly where white in mating captured neither of the black checking men. No. 7 by the three Bettmanns, the two brothers and their cousin, with its thematic key, is a beautiful example of this task.

Other problems composed primarily to illustrate cross-checking are Nos. 92, 93, 121, 123 and 159. Two cross-checking variations are changed in No. 128. No. 91 shows three cross-checking lines blended with three mates by discovered check from moves of white's queen's pawn. Blends of cross-checks with other thematic elements are shown with half-pins in Rothstein's No. 65 and White's classic No. 68. Interesting cross-checks also occur in Nos. 4, 60 and 98.

Various forms of pinning and unpinning, frequently in combination, provide the motif for many modern two-movers, and in numerous other instances are blended with other strategic elements, especially since the flowering of the half-pin in Good Companion days.

Unpins of white by the interference of a black man on the line of pin is the principal feature in many fine compositions in the collection, such as Nos. 44, 100 and 155. Unpinning of the white rook is the most conspicuous element in the elaborate structure of Gamage's No. 165. Vinje's No. 124, already referred to in connection with Grimshaw interferences, is an example of unpinning by the *withdrawal* of the black pinning pieces.

No. 83 was composed to show simultaneous unpinning of both the white and black queens, tripled. In No. 145 the white queen and a black knight are twice unpinned simultaneously, while there is a third unpin of the white queen only.

In the Howard theme, illustrated in problems No. 81 and No. 84, the keymove, by a line-pinned white piece, unpins a black man, which in turn unpins the key-piece by interference, allowing it to mate.

In the Dalton theme, illustrated in No. 85, the keymove unpins a black man (the knight), which then pins its unpinner (the queen) in the thematic line. No. 85 complicates this maneuver by combining it with the reverse procedure, since the keymove also self-pins white's queen's knight, which is then unpinned by black's king's knight so it can mate, the combined effect being shown in the thematic variation 1 Q g3, Sg2; 2 Se4.

There are four ways by which either a black or a white man may become self-pinned. In many problems that feature the unpinning of a white man, the thematic keymove is one that self-pins the white man which is to be unpinned by black defensive moves. Such is the key of No. 165, where the withdrawal of white's king's rook off the fifth rank leaves the queen's rook pinned. This actually is an example of a white half-pin. The problems discussed in the following paragraphs, however, are all ones in which black men are self-pinned.

The first way in which a black man may become self-pinned is by capturing a white man on a line between the black king and a long-range white piece. A typical example of this type of self-pinning occurs in problem No. 7.

A second way is by the movement of the black king himself onto the line of pin. This may occur by the capture of a white man by the king.

A third way is by the interposition of a black man on a line of check. In a two-move problem this would require a checking key. Recently some attention has been given to effects that may be secured through the employment of checking keys in two-movers, but ordinarily this form of self-pinning is of practical importance only in three-movers and longer problems.

The fourth way is one that plays a major role in a great number of modern two-movers. In the initial position two black men are on a line between the black king and a long-range white piece. The withdrawal of either black man from the line leaves its fellow self-pinned. As previously mentioned such an arrangement is termed a "half-pin," which is illustrated in a beautifully simple setting in Promislo's No. 77. The term is commonly applied only where the pinning is essential to white's mating move.

One prominent application of black self-pinning by capture is in the theme known as the Schiffmann Defense. In this theme white threatens mate by discovery from a battery, and in the thematic defense black self-pins a man in such a manner that if white makes the threat move the firing piece of the battery will unpin the self-pinned black man, so it can defeat the threat. This is illustrated in No. 98, as mentioned in the preceding chapter. White plays 1 Qg1, threatening mate by 2 Pf4. Black can defend by 1 — — P × S, self-pinning the pawn. Should white now persist in playing 2 Pf4 ck, the black pawn would be unpinned and could interpose, 2 — — Pe3. So white must change his mating move to 2 Pf3.

With an excellent flight-yielding key, Kish triples the Schiffmann Defense in his No. 117. It has been shown in fourfold renderings by several composers, but frequently these extreme versions become mechanical and less pleasing aesthetically than where the composer does not strive to attain task limits.

What is known as a Secondary Schiffmann Defense is the theme of Buchwald's No. 180. In this problem, after black makes a thematic self-pinning capture, the threatened mating move, 2 Pb5, would not unpin the self-pinned black man, but it no longer would be a mate because by the capture black removes an essential guard of c5. The point of No. 180 lies in the differentiation of the mates according to which black man captures white's queen's pawn: 1 Qa4, B × P; 2 Pe4 (not Se4): 1 — — P × P; 2 Se4 (not 2 Pe4): 1 — — S × P; 2 Qa2 (not 2 Pe4 nor 2 Se4).

Self-pinning by withdrawal, the fourth way by which a black man may become self-pinned, can arise from a wide variety of arrangements of half-pinned men. A half-pin is termed "complete" when the withdrawal of *either* of the half-pinned pair results in a mate which would be prevented by the unmoved black man were it not pinned. Such a mate is called a pin-mate. If the withdrawal of only one of a half-pinned pair leads to a pin-mate the half-pin is termed "incomplete." Few incomplete half-pins are seen in modern two-movers.

No. 77 illustrates half-pinning in simple form, combined with no other elements except a self-block in one line of play. After the keymove, 1 Qc7, if 1 — — Sd7; 2 Qc4, and 1 — — QS else; 2 Qc8. In each mate black's king's knight is essentially pinned. Then if 1 — — KS any; 2 Pd5, and black's queen's knight is essentially pinned. So the half-pin is of the complete type, because a move of either knight leads to a pin-mate based on the unmoved knight.

Half-pins are known as homogeneous if both half-pinned men are of the same kind, i.e., two rooks or two bishops; heterogeneous if the men are of different kinds, i.e., a pawn and a rook, or a queen and a knight. Examples of homogeneous half-pinned pairs appear in Nos. 65, 75, 77, 78, 89, 112 and 168; of heterogeneous pairs in Nos. 68, 87, 120 and 125.

An odd type of half-pin is featured in Sheppard's No. 78; two pawns half-pinned *vertically* above the black king. The half-pinning of two pawns on the same rank as the king is quite common, but it would be impossible to show a complete half-pin with two pawns pinned vertically below the king or with two pawns pinned diagonally. In either of such cases if the pawn nearer the king moved off the line of pin, no pin-mate could be arranged in which the pinning of the further pawn would be an essential factor.

Another unusual type of half-pin occurs in the attractive No. 168, where two rooks are half-pinned horizontally.

One of the reasons that half-pins are so popular with composers and are found in so many fine problems is because they can so readily be blended with other thematic elements. Nos. 65 and 68 show half-pins with cross-checks. No. 75 blends half-pinning with interferences on the black queen and bishop; and No. 120 both with interferences and self-blocks.

As defined by Alain White in *Changing Fashions*, the Hume theme "involves two pinned white pieces, each to be unpinned in turn by an interference move made by one of two black half-pinned pieces, leading to true half-pin mates by the unpinned white men." In the Inverted Hume theme, "The black half-pin is here, but instead of white unpinning, we get white pinning." The Inverted Hume theme is illustrated in Nos. 87 and 89. In the former the thematic variations are: 1 Qd4,

Pb3; 2 Sb5, and 1 — — Sc4; 2 Qc3. In the latter:
QS any; 2 Sb4, and 1 — — Sc5; 2 Q × P.

Composers are continually exploring the possibil
further combinations of pinning and unpinning, of whic
new types are shown in Nos. 167 and 171. There a
thematic variations in No. 167. The key, 1 Rc5, unp
black queen and at the same time pins white's queen's
To defeat the threat, 2 Rd5, black may play 1 — — Q
1 — — Q × KS, in either case self-pinning the black que
unpinning white's queen's knight, which then plays resp
2 Sc4 or 2 Se4, each of which is a pin-mate.

Sheppard's No. 171 is an elaboration of the Dalton
The key, 1 Qe4, unpins the black knight, any move o
then pins the white queen, which constitutes the Dalton
1 — — Sd6 enriches the play by unpinning the white
permitting mate by 2 Be6.

Although there is not nearly so wide a field for
promotion play in the two-mover as in longer pr
American composers have produced some beautiful tw
compositions based on pawn-promotion motifs. The
of the two-move problem does not permit of differe
between white pawn promotion to queen or to rook or
except as a keymove. On the mating move the only di
that can be shown is between promotion to queen or to
since the queen can always give the same mates as a ro
bishop.

Dr. Bettmann's No. 79 shows the promotion of a sing
pawn either to queen or knight on three different s
according to black's play, producing six thematic var
With an odd, flight-yielding key, Sheppard, in his
shows pawn promotion to knight on three different sq
a Meredith setting. Two white pawns provide four n
promotion in No. 101, two of them being pin-mate
essential pinning of the black queen.

Modern Trends

FROM time to time during the last half-century various chess problem critics have predicted the approaching exhaustion of the two-move problem. Yet whenever currently popular forms of the two-mover have tended to become threadbare through tiresome repetition, new thematic types have been suggested by the more imaginative composers. Features in which today's problemists are chiefly interested received but scant attention, or even were unrecognized, four or five decades ago.

For example, line openings and closings occur as incidental features in many problems of earlier years, but only in more recent days have they been treated as a definite theme, culminating in four-way play, often shown in multiple form.

In black's defensive play the stress is now laid principally on the relationship between different black moves, especially when made by the same piece. This is shown in the composing of problems specifically to illustrate correction play, third degree mechanisms and chain progressions. Other modern thematic types are compositions that feature dual avoidance on the mating move, or which illustrate reciprocal changed-mate play.

The collection includes numerous problems in which line opening or closing ranges from a single striking line-opening variation to complex multiple effects. An early thematic single line opening for white is shown dramatically in the theme that Loyd called The American Indian. No. 58 is a simplification of Loyd's bizarre diagonal version published in 1889, to which he first applied the name. Kennard's No. 54 is another fine diagonal rendering; Nos. 16 and 119 are horizontal versions; and a vertical one is shown in Hassberg's miniature, No. 179.

A variety of forms of line opening and closing are illustrated in Nos. 110, 146 and 155. Echoed black line openings for white, permitting self-interference mates, are the heart of Gamage's beautiful No. 146. In No. 155 the variations 1 Sg6, Sc6; and 1 — — KSc4, are examples of simultaneous closing of both white and black lines, while 1 — — QSc4 closes one white and two black lines. Finally in Kish's No. 110, composed to illustrate white pawn-one-two play, the variation 1 Qg2, Rd3, also has a three-way effect in that black's move opens one black line and closes both a black and a white line.

Valves and Bivalves, the 1930 volume in Alain White's *Christmas Series*, was devoted to problems in which a black man made a defensive move that in opening a line for a long-range black piece closed another black line of influence, a two-way procedure.

A further elaboration of such line studies led to combinations in which both black and white pieces were simultaneously involved, and later many problems were composed to exhibit what has been termed Four-Way Play. In this maneuver, a black man, in making a defensive move, opens both a black line and a white line, and at the same time closes both a black line and a white line, producing a four-way effect. Problems have been constructed in which two or three variations illustrate this play, such as Sheppard's No. 176.

In No. 85, 1 — — Sg2 actually has a five-way effect since it closes two black lines, b2 - h2 and h1 - a8, opens the black line d6 - h2, closes the white line g1 - g7, and opens the white line g3 - e5.

In *A Century of Two-Movers*, the first volume in Frank Altschul's chess problem series, dual avoidance is defined on page 205 as follows: "dual avoidance implies the presence in a problem of two or more variations with Black defences of a similar kind, which in each case seem to allow two mates, also of a similar kind, but one of them is avoided in an artistic manner. For the theme to stand out clearly, the method of suppressing the duals should be similar in both variations and it should not depend directly upon the Black defence, but upon some additional function of the black force. ... the impending dual of one variation may be realized in the actual play of the second variation, and *vice versa*."

An example of dual avoidance occurs in No. 82. After the key, 1 Sc3, white threatens 2 Se2, but this mate can be prevented by any move of the black bishop, vacating d5, so that the white knight must maintain its guard on that square. Random moves of the bishop along the a2 - g8 diagonal lead to mate by 2 Re4, and random moves along the a8 - h1 diagonal are followed by 2 Rc4. 1 — — Bc4 and 1 — — Be4, however, would seem to permit mate by either rook until it is perceived that these bishop moves cut off the guard on d3 of the white bishop and queen respectively, and so determine white's mating move.

Quoting further from *A Century of Two-Movers*: "there are two principal methods of introducing, and at the same time suppressing, faulty or potential play. One method is dual avoidance, which has already been discussed. The second method is the *Contingent Threat*, with the thematic *Black Corrections* it involves." On page 170 these terms are explained thus: "In a threat problem, if the removal of a Black piece away from its original square in itself defeats the threat, irrespective of where it is moved to, yet at the same time permits a new threat to become effective against purposeless moves of the Black piece, such a secondary threat is called a *Contingent Threat* and any defensive moves of the Black piece which defeat this contingent threat, as well as the original threat, are called *Black Corrections*."

While black correction play occurs as a secondary element in many problems, it may be made the outstanding feature of a composition. Black correction play is distinctly the theme of Kish's No. 118, where the initial threat is defeated by any random move of either black knight. Black's king's knight can make three corrections to defeat the contingent threat of 2 Q × Q. Random moves of black's queen's knight lead to the contingent threat 2 Qb5, and this knight can make two correction moves.

In Sheppard's elaborate No. 176 black corrections and four-way play are so artistically blended that neither seems dominant. The black corrections are 1 — — Sc3 and 1 — — Se5, both of which have four-way effects.

Following the publication of *Variation Play*, much attention was given to the composition of what Jacobs and White described as the *Third Degree Mechanism*. "Is it possible to present a Black move which will pass unscathed through the Third

Degree inquisition of an initial threat, a removal threat and an arrival threat, and emerge with simultaneous offsets to them all, leading to a final mixed variation mate? . . . Our test, then, for a Third Degree threat play will be on the one hand that the complete removal of a Black unit from its original square will permit a removal threat to function, and on the other hand that the occupation of one square, or of two or more related squares, by a Black dummy will permit an arrival threat to function, but that a move of the particular Black unit to one of the squares under consideration will offset both the removal threat and the arrival threat, as well as the initial threat, if any, with the desirable by-play that a move of this Black unit to another of the related squares will allow the arrival threat to operate, so that the contrast between the arrival threat and the offset may be clearly set forth."

Such third degree play is brilliantly illustrated in Hassberg's No. 174. The key, 1 Rc5, sets up the initial threat, 2 Bb7. Any random move of the black rook defeats this threat, but leads to the removal threat, 2 Bd3. An incidental attractive feature is that the initial and removal threats are made by the same white piece. Black defends against both the initial threat and the removal threat by 1 — — Rd4, but white now mates by the arrival threat, 2 Q × P. Finally, black can defend all three threats—initial, removal and arrival—by 1 — — Rc3, a triple offset, and white then mates by 2 Qd4.

Another excellent example of third degree mechanism is shown in No. 184; and the play is doubled in No. 191, considering the moves of both black knights in each of the thematic sequences.

No. 182 is a pioneer example of a mechanism developed by Eaton, which he aptly christened Chain Progression. Chain Progression occurs when a black piece can make a series of defensive moves in which two of such moves make a related pair because of certain similarities in their effects, and then one of the pair makes a second pair with a third move of the piece because of other similarities in their effects.

Thus in No. 182, after the key, 1 Q × P, the initial threat is 2 Rf6. Any random move of black's queen's knight defeats this threat but permits 2 S × B, a contingent threat, to offset which the black knight can make three correction moves,

1 — — Sd7, 1 — — Sc6 and 1 — — Sc4. 1 — — Sd7 and
1 — — Sc6 form a related pair because they permit and offset
the arrival threat 2 Pe8 = Q. 1 — — Sc6 and 1 — — Sc4
form a second related pair because they permit and offset the
second arrival threat of 2 Qd6. The defense 1 — — Sc6 is
the linking move in the progression.

Eaton's No. 188 illustrates another type of progression: a
four-step progression, with initial threat, removal threat, arrival
threat, and arrival threat with an added factor. Following
the key, 1 Se1, the initial threat is 2 Sg2. This is defeated by
any random move of the black knight (1 — — S × B or
1 — — Sc7), when the removal threat, 2 Pd5, functions. Both
initial and removal threats are offset by 1 — — Se3, which
permits the arrival threat 2 Se2. 1 — — Sc3 again offsets
the initial and the removal threats, and although it unpins
white's king's knight it prevents the latter from mating because
it guards e2, *an added factor*. Its interference on the black rook,
however, takes the guard off d3 and white mates by 2 Sd3.
1 — — Se7 and 1 — — Sf6 make another similar pair of
defenses with related arrival threats, thus doubling the illustration of the theme. There is also a fifth black correction,
unrelated to the others, 1 — — Sb6, met by 2 Bd6.

Another modern development is the study of various forms
of reciprocal play. Hassberg's No. 173 is an example of
reciprocations in black corrections. Following a key, 1 Se3,
that yields two flights to the black king, the initial threat is
2 S × S. This threat is defeated by any move of either black
knight. A random move of the knight on c4 is met by 2 S × P;
and when black makes the correction move 1 — — Sd6, white
mates by 2 Sg4. Any random move of the knight on c5 is
met by 2 Sg4; whereas after the correction move 1 — — S × P
white mates by 2 S × P. Thus the mate after a random move
of one black piece is the same as that after a correction move of
a companion black piece, and vice versa.

No. 185 shows similar reciprocal play. After random moves
of the black knight on e3 the mate is 2 Sb6; after the correction
move 1 — — S × Sd5, the mate is 2 Sb2. These mates are
transposed following random moves of the knight on e5
and its correction move, 1 — — Sd3.

In No. 193 a reciprocal change is shown between potential and actual play.   As set, after 1 — — Kd3, white can mate by 2 Sb4; and after 1 — — Ke5, by 2 Sf4.   In the solution these mates are transposed, following the key 1 Sd4.

A different form of reciprocal play appears in No. 199.   In the initial position, if 1 — — B × Sf6, white mates by 2 Re3; and   if   1 — — S × Sf6,   by   2 Re7.   After   the   key,   if 1 — — B × Sf4,   then   white   mates   by   2 Re7;   and   after 1 — — S × Sf4, by 2 Re3.

A related form of reciprocal play is exhibited in Alain White's No. 149, where there are four set mates from one pawn in the initial position, while in the actual play four mates are given by another pawn.

THE COLLECTION

White to Play

and Mate in Two Moves

Note

THE PROBLEMS that follow are arranged in chronological order of publication, as nearly as the author has been able to ascertain the publication dates. Since only two-movers are included in the collection, it is considered unnecessary to insert under each individual diagram the stipulation "White to play and mate in two moves." The letter "V" where it appears before the source of publication indicates that the position is a revised version of the problem as originally published.

The notation used in the text and solutions is a form of the *algebraic*, commonly used in books on problems because it is more concise and exact than the *English* notation. In the algebraic notation the locations and moves of the men are always read from the white side of the board, or the lower side of the diagram. From left to right the files are designated "a" to "h," and the ranks are numbered "1" to "8" reading upward.

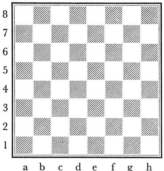

The same letters are used to denote the men as in the English notation, with the exception of S (German *Springer*) for knight. The symbol × is used for captures; the symbol = for pawn promotion, followed by a letter to show the piece selected.

Readers who would like to follow some definite procedure in solving problems may be interested in the methods suggested in the author's *How To Solve Chess Problems* (Dover).

Samuel Loyd
V Boston Gazette
1859

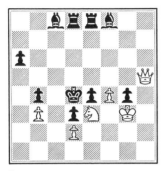

1

George E. Carpenter
First Prize
Dubuque Chess Journal
1871

2

William A. Shinkman
First Prize
Huddersfield College Magazine
October, 1877

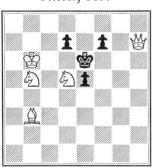

3

Charles A. Gilberg
First Prize
Danbury News
1877

4

Jesse A. Graves
American Chess Journal
1878

5

William A. Shinkman
Detroit Free Press
c. 1880

6

Henry W., Edgar and
Jacob Bettmann
Quebec Chronicle
1882

7

Henry W. and
Edgar Bettmann
South Australian Chronicle
1883

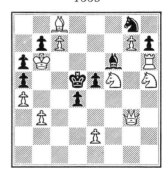

8

William Meredith
Dubuque Chess Journal
November, 1886

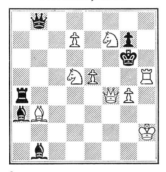

9

William Meredith
Dubuque Chess Journal
December, 1886

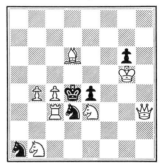

10

Benjamin S. Wash
Second Prize
Nashville American
1887

11

Henry W. and
Edgar Bettmann
Second Prize
Nashville American
1887

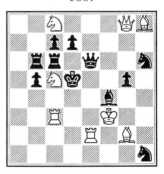

12

Benjamin S. Wash
Sunny South
September, 1888

Henry W. and
Edgar Bettmann
First Prize
St. John's Globe
1888

13

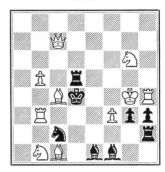

14

William Meredith
First Prize, Ninth Tourney
Dubuque Chess Journal
December, 1889

Samuel Loyd
New York State Chess
Association
February 22, 1892

15

16

Otto Wurzburg
V First Prize
Philadelphia Herald
1893

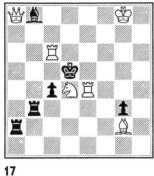

17

Joseph N. Babson
New Orleans Times-Democrat
May 21, 1893

18

Samuel M. Joseph
First Prize
Brighton Society
1895

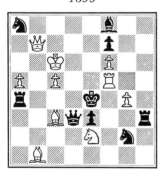

19

Samuel Loyd
New York Commercial Advertiser
1897

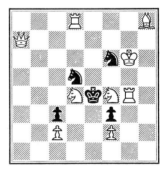

20

Otto Wurzburg
American Chess Magazine
1898

21

Henry W. Barry
First Prize
La Stratégie
1901

22

Joseph C. J. Wainwright
(*Les Tours de Force No. 170*)
1902

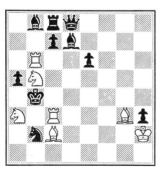

23

David T. Brock
Second Prize
The Literary Digest
1903

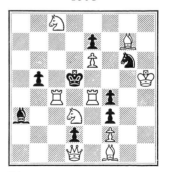

24

Kenneth S. Howard
Second Prize
Revue d'Echecs
1904

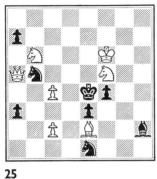

25

Walter I. Kennard
Checkmate
February, 1904

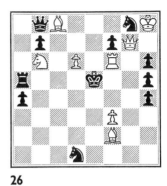

26

Kenneth S. Howard
Checkmate
September, 1904

27

Joseph C. J. Wainwright
(*Les Tours de Force No. 14*)
1906

28

Murray Marble
La Stratégie
September, 1907

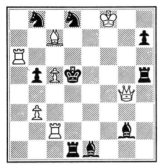

29

Murray Marble
First Prize
La Stratégie
1908–1909

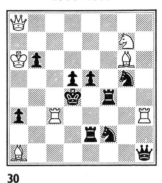

30

Louis H. Jokisch
Tidskrift för Schack
1909

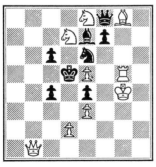

31

Murray Marble
American Chess Bulletin
March, 1910

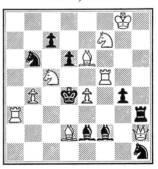

32

William A. Shinkman
American Chess Bulletin
October, 1910

33

William A. Shinkman
V Westen und Daheim
1910

34

F. Gamage
V First Prize
Illustreret Familien Journal
1910

35

F. Gamage
First Prize
Tidskrift för Schack
1911

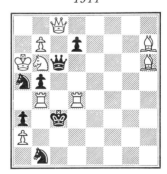

36

A. J. Fink
First Prize
American Chess Bulletin
1913

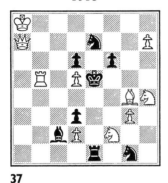

37

A. J. Fink
First Prize
Szachista Polski
1913

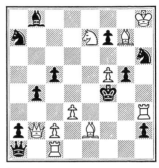

38

William B. Rice
Der Westen
November 9, 1913

39

William B. Rice
Good Companions
April, 1914

40

Charles Promislo
Second Prize
Good Companions
December, 1914

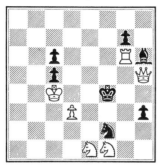

41

Otto Wurzburg
(after Loyd, 1876)
The White King
1914

42

F. Gamage
First Prize
Tidskrift för Schack
1914

43

Murray Marble
British Chess Magazine
January, 1915

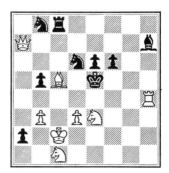

44

Charles Promislo
First Honorable Mention
Good Companions
February 22, 1915

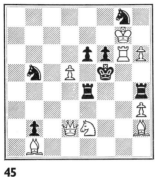

45

William B. Rice
First Prize
First Meredith Tourney
Good Companions
May, 1915

46

Gilbert Dobbs
Fourth Prize
First Meredith Tourney
Good Companions
May, 1915

47

William B. Rice
Good Companions
May, 1915

48

Henry Wald Bettmann
Der Westen
July 18, 1915

49

Charles Promislo
Second Prize
Good Companions
February 22, 1916

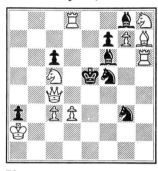

50

A. J. Fink
Good Companions
February, 1917

51

William B. Rice
Third Prize
Good Companions
April, 1917

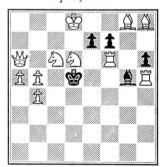

52

Otto Wurzburg
First Prize, Eighth Tourney
Pittsburgh Gazette-Times
June 10, 1917

53

Walter I. Kennard
(Quoted) Boston Transcript
August 14, 1917

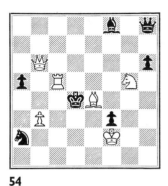

54

William B. Rice
First Prize
Good Companions
January, 1918

55

Henry Wald Bettmann
First Prize
Good Companions
February 22, 1918

56

Alain White
First Prize
Seventh Meredith Tourney
Good Companions
May, 1918

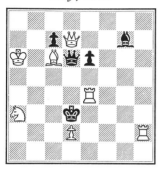

57

Frank Janet
(after Loyd, 1889)
British Chess Magazine
September, 1918

58

John F. Barry
Good Companions
February 22, 1919

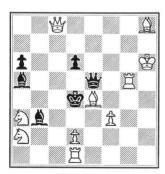

59

Lewis Rothstein
First Prize
Good Companions
February, 1919

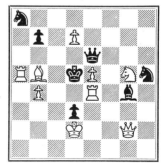

60

R. E. L. Windle
Second Prize
Ninth Meredith Tourney
Good Companions
April, 1919

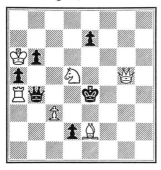

61

Gilbert Dobbs
Second Prize
Tenth Meredith Tourney
Good Companions
October, 1919

62

Charles Promislo
Second Prize
Boston Transcript
1919

63

Gilbert Dobbs
Honorable Mention
Boston Transcript
1919

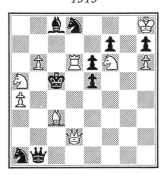

64

Lewis Rothstein
Good Companions
January, 1920

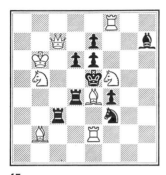

65

A. J. Fink
Third Honorable Mention
Good Companions
February, 1920

66

A. J. Fink
Good Companions
February, 1920

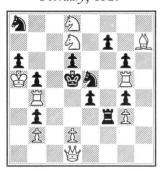

67

Alain White
Good Companions
March, 1920

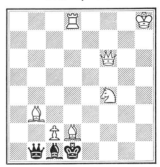

68

Charles Promislo
Good Companions
April, 1920

69

A. J. Fink and Ua Tane
First Prize
Good Companions
July, 1920

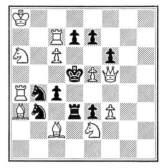

70

Charles W. Sheppard
Third Prize
Thirteenth Meredith Tourney
Good Companions
March, 1921

71

A. J. Fink
First Prize, Meredith Class
Third Complete Block Tourney
Good Companions
April, 1921

72.

Henry Wald Bettmann
V Good Companions
April, 1921

73

Henry Wald Bettmann
Second Prize
Good Companions
May, 1921

74

A. J. Fink
Honorable Mention
Eighth American Chess Congress
1921

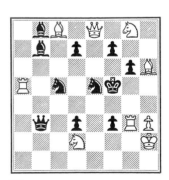

75

Charles Promislo
Second Prize, Meredith Section
Eighth American Chess Congress
Good Companions
August, 1921

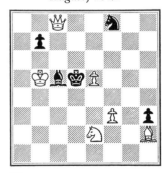

76

Charles Promislo
Third Honorable Mention
Meredith Section
Eighth American Chess Congress
Good Companions, August, 1921

77

Charles W. Sheppard
Good Companions
October, 1921

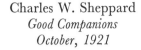
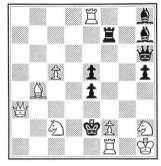

78

Henry Wald Bettmann
Good Companions
January, 1923

79

William B. Rice
The Pittsburgh Post
April 29, 1923

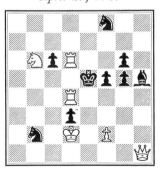

80

Kenneth S. Howard
and Alain White
L'Alfiere di Re
October-November, 1925

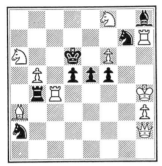

81

Kenneth S. Howard
V L'Alfiere di Re
October-November, 1925

82

Kenneth S. Howard
The Pittsburgh Post
November 8, 1925

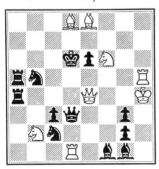

83

Kenneth S. Howard
The Empire Review
January, 1926

84

Kenneth S. Howard
V Bristol Times and Mirror
August 28, 1926

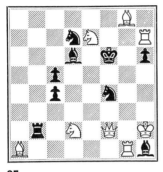

85

Kenneth S. Howard
The Observer
November 21, 1926

86

Kenneth S. Howard
The Observer
December 26, 1927

87

Reginald B. Cooke
Illustrated London News
1929

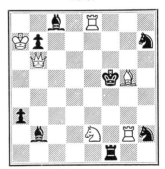

88

Kenneth S. Howard
First Prize
Die Schwalbe
First Quarter, 1929

89

Vincent L. Eaton
Cincinnati Enquirer
1930

90

Kenneth S. Howard
First Prize
The Western Morning News
July-December, 1932

91

Kenneth S. Howard
Dagens Nyheder
October 30, 1932

92

Vaux Wilson
First Prize
Cincinnati Enquirer
November 13, 1932

93

Geoffrey Mott-Smith
New York Sun
1932

94

Walter Jacobs
British Chess Magazine
January, 1933

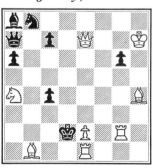

95

A. J. Fink
V The Chess Review
September, 1933

96

Geoffrey Mott-Smith
Boston Transcript
September 12, 1933

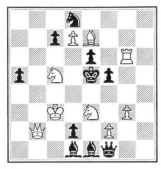

97

Kenneth S. Howard
Third Honorable Mention
The Western Morning News
July-December, 1933

98

Kenneth S. Howard
Grand Rapids Herald
December 3, 1933

99

Alexander Kish
Cincinnati Enquirer
April 28, 1934

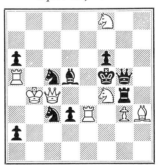

100

Kenneth S. Howard
Skakbladet
April, 1934

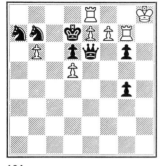

101

Alexander Kish
Cincinnati Enquirer
July 7, 1934

102

William A. Beers
Atlanta Journal
September 14, 1934

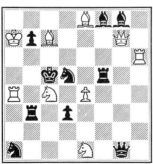

103

Vincent L. Eaton
First Prize
Cleveland vs. Cincinnati
Solving Contest
September, 1934

104

Kenneth S. Howard
Cleveland vs. Cincinnati
Solving Contest
September, 1934

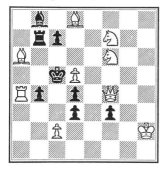

105

Gilbert Dobbs
Minneapolis Journal
1934

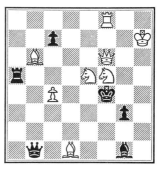

106

Geoffrey Mott-Smith
The Chess Review
April, 1935

107

Alexander Kish
First Honorable Mention
Pawn-One-Two Tourney
American Chess Bulletin
1935-1936

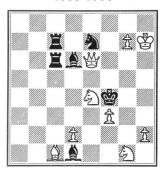

108

Patrick Moran
Fourth Commended
Pawn-One-Two Tourney
American Chess Bulletin
1935-1936

109

Alexander Kish
Sixth Commended
Pawn-One-Two Tourney
American Chess Bulletin
1935-1936

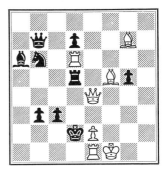

110

Alexander Kish
The Christian Science Monitor
July 23, 1935

1.11

Alexander Kish
Cincinnati Enquirer
September 1, 1935

112

H. L. Winings
Cincinnati Enquirer
November 10, 1935

113

Alexander Kish
The Christian Science Monitor
November 19, 1935

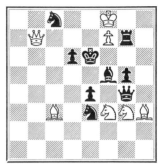

114

Alexander Kish
The Emery Memorial
1936

115

Otto Wurzburg
American Chess Bulletin
January, 1936

116

Alexander Kish
American Chess Bulletin
January, 1936

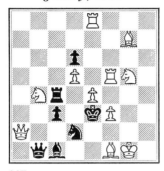

117

Alexander Kish
Cincinnati Enquirer
April 12, 1936

118

Vincent L. Eaton
Melbourne Leader
1936

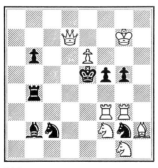

119

Vincent L. Eaton
Second Prize
Open Section, C. C. L. A.
North American Tourney, 1936

120

Alexander Kish
First Prize
Cross-Check Section
C. C. L. A.
North American Tourney, 1936

121

Geoffrey Mott-Smith
The Chess Review
December, 1937

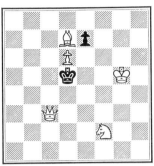

122

F. Gamage
First Prize
Cross-Check Section
C. C. L. A.
North American Tourney, 1937

123

Oscar E. Vinje
The Observer
January 30, 1938

124

V. Rosado
The Chess Review
February, 1938

125

F. Gamage
C. C. L. A. Bulletin
March, 1938

126

Kenneth S. Howard
American Chess Bulletin
July-August, 1938

127

Kenneth S. Howard
American Chess Bulletin
January-February, 1939

128

F. Gamage
Honor Problem
The Chess Review
February, 1939

129

William A. Beers
First Prize
American Chess Bulletin
Informal Tourney, 1939

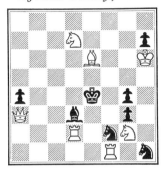

130

F. Gamage
Honor Problem
The Chess Review
April, 1939

131

Otto Wurzburg
American Chess Bulletin
July-August, 1939

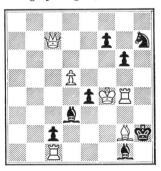

132

Otto Wurzburg
The Atlanta Journal
September 29, 1939

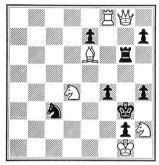

133

Edgar Theimer
American Chess Bulletin
September-October, 1939

134

Alexander Kish
American Chess Bulletin
September-October, 1939

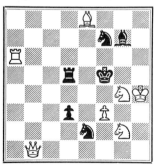

135

Geoffrey Mott-Smith
The Chess Review
November, 1939

136

F. Gamage
Mitteldeutsche Zeitung
1939

137

F. Gamage
V Third Prize
Open Section, C. C. L. A.
North American Tourney, 1939

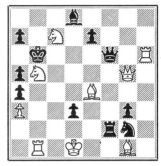

138

Gilbert Dobbs
First Commended
Mutate Section, C. C. L. A.
North American Tourney, 1939

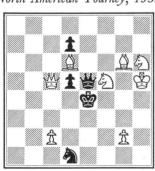

139

Vincent L. Eaton
The Chess Review
April, 1940

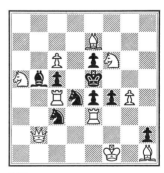

140

F. Gamage
First Prize
American Chess Bulletin
Informal Tourney, 1940

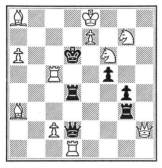

141

Eugene Neuhaus
American Chess Bulletin
September-October, 1940

142

Gilbert Dobbs
Second Honorable Mention
(ex æquo)
British Chess Magazine
July-December, 1940

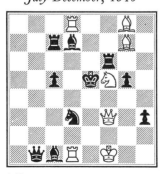

143

F. Gamage
First Prize
John Keeble Memorial Tourney
The Falkirk Herald
1940

144

F. Gamage
Third Prize
John Keeble Memorial Tourney
The Falkirk Herald, 1940

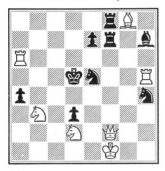

145

F. Gamage
First Honorable Mention
American Chess Bulletin
Informal Tourney, 1941

146

F. Gamage
The Chess Review
April, 1941

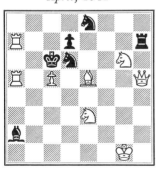

147

F. Gamage
The Washington Star
September 24, 1941

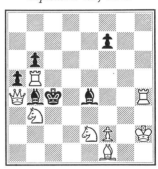

148

Alain White
American Chess Bulletin
November-December, 1941

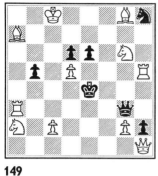

149

F. Gamage
First Prize, Meredith Tourney
The Chess Correspondent
November, 1941

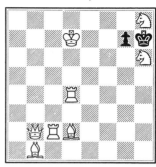

150

F. Gamage
The Philadelphia Inquirer
1941

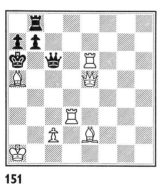

151

F. Gamage
First Prize
The Falkirk Herald
1941

152

Eric M. Hassberg
First Honorable Mention
The Washington Star
January 25, 1942

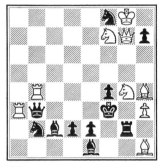

153

G. F. Rose
Third Prize, Meredith Tourney
The Chess Correspondent
February, 1942

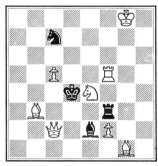

154

F. Gamage
First Prize, First Tourney
The Christian Science Monitor
March 14, 1942

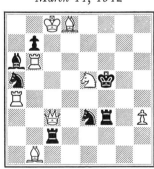

155

Geoffrey Mott-Smith
V American Chess Bulletin
March-April, 1942

156

Edgar Holladay
American Chess Bulletin
November-December, 1942

157

Geoffrey Mott-Smith
American Chess Bulletin
November-December, 1942

158

Otto Wurzburg
Third Honorable Mention
American Chess Bulletin
Informal Tourney, 1942

159

Charles W. Sheppard
The Chess Correspondent
January, 1943

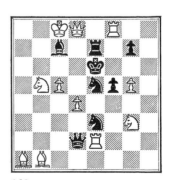

160

Otto Wurzburg
The Chess Correspondent
January, 1943

Charles W. Sheppard
First Honorable Mention
American Chess Bulletin
Informal Tourney, 1943

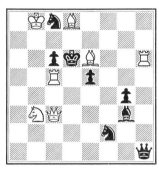

161

162

Geoffrey Mott-Smith
Chess Review
March, 1943

George B. Spencer
First Prize, Decalet Tourney
Chess Review
April, 1943

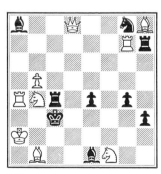

163

164

F. Gamage
First Prize
American Chess Bulletin
Informal Tourney, 1943

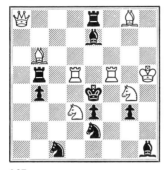

165

Edgar Holladay
Third Commended
American Chess Bulletin
Informal Tourney, 1943

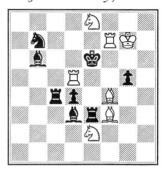

166

F. Gamage
First Prize
N, PS/N, PS-Pin Tourney
British Chess Magazine
January, 1944

167

Walter Jacobs
First Prize
American Chess Bulletin
Informal Tourney, 1944

168

Edgar Holladay
Second Honorable Mention
American Chess Bulletin
Informal Tourney, 1944

169

Charles W. Sheppard
First Commended
American Chess Bulletin
Informal Tourney, 1944

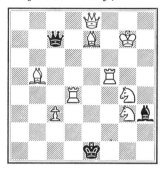

170

Charles W. Sheppard
Second Commended
American Chess Bulletin
Informal Tourney, 1944

171

F. Gamage
Honor Problem
The Chess Correspondent
July, 1944

172

Eric M. Hassberg
Second Prize
Xadrez Brasileiro
Theme Tourney, July, 1944

173

Eric M. Hassberg
Third Honorable Mention
American Chess Bulletin
Informal Tourney, 1944

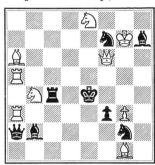

174

Newman Guttman
Third Honorable Mention
Third Hochberg Memorial
Tourney
The Chess Correspondent, 1944

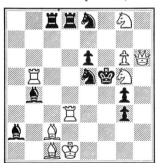

175

Charles W. Sheppard
V First Honorable Mention
American Chess Bulletin
Informal Tourney, 1944

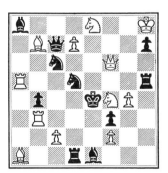

176

A. J. Fink
First Honorable Mention
American Chess Bulletin
Informal Tourney, 1945

177

Joe Youngs
" *To Alain White* "
March 3, 1945

178

Eric M. Hassberg
New York Post
April 21, 1945

179

Julius Buchwald
First Prize
American Chess Bulletin
Informal Tourney, 1945

180

Edgar Holladay
V Fourth Commended
American Chess Bulletin
Informal Tourney, 1945

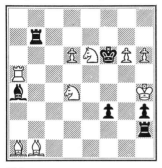

181

Vincent L. Eaton
American Chess Bulletin
May-June, 1946

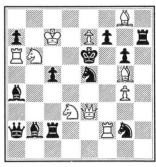

182

Julius Buchwald
First Prize
American Chess Bulletin
Informal Tourney, 1946

183

Walter B. Suesman
Specially Commended, 3° Tourney
The Chess Correspondent
July-August, 1946

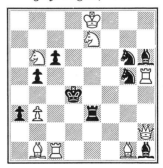

184

Eric M. Hassberg
New York Post
October 26, 1946

185

Julius Buchwald
First Prize
Enroque!
1946

186

Francis J. C. DeBlasio
First Prize, Tourney No. 1
The United States
Chess Federation
1946

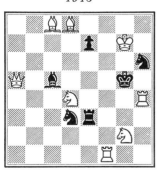

187

Vincent L. Eaton
V Second Prize, Tourney No. 1
The United States
Chess Federation
1946

188

Julius Buchwald
Parallele 50
January 17, 1948

189

Joe Youngs
The Christian Science Monitor
April 17, 1948

190

Newman Guttman
First Prize, 3º Tourney
The Chess Correspondent
1947-1948

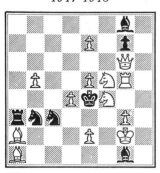

191

Edgar Holladay
Second Honorable Mention
British Chess Federation
Tourney No. 60, 1948-1949

192

Eric M. Hassberg
First Prize
Olympic Tourney
1948-1950

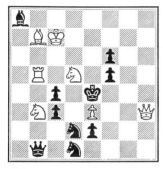

193

F. Gamage
Third Prize
Max Feigl Memorial Tourney
1948-1950

194

Kenneth S. Howard
American Chess Bulletin
January-February, 1949

195

Nicholas Gabor
Highly Commended
The Christian Science Monitor
1949

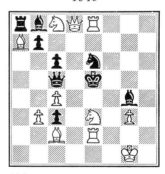

196

Edgar Holladay
Third Prize
British Chess Magazine
1951

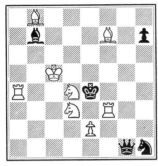

197

Charles W. Sheppard
Third Prize
American Chess Bulletin
Informal Tourney, 1951

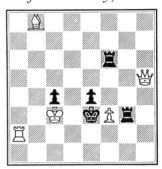

198

Eric M. Hassberg
Fourth Prize
Gross Memorial Tourney
1951

199

Charles W. Sheppard
First Prize
American Chess Bulletin
Informal Tourney, 1952

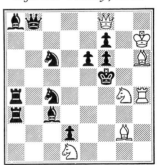

200

Francis J. C. DeBlasio
American Chess Bulletin
November-December, 1952

201

B. M. Berd
Honorable Mention
American Chess Bulletin
Informal Tourney, 1953

202

Charles W. Sheppard
American Chess Bulletin
March-April, 1954

203

Vaux Wilson
American Chess Bulletin
July-August, 1955

204

Robert E. Burger
First Prize
American Chess Bulletin
Informal Tourney, 1955

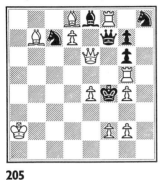

205

Robert E. Burger
American Chess Bulletin
November-December, 1955

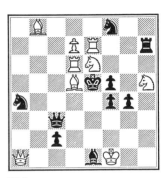

206

Newman Guttman
Third Prize, Section I
Chess Life
1955-1956

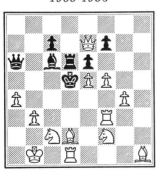

207

Robert E. Burger
First Prize, Section II
Chess Life
1955-1956

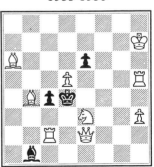

208

Charles W. Sheppard
Commended, Section II
Chess Life
1955-1956

209

Edgar Holladay
American Chess Bulletin
March-April, 1956

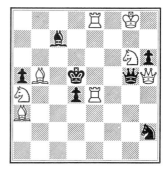

210

Edgar Holladay
American Chess Bulletin
September-October, 1957

211

William L. Barclay
American Chess Bulletin
May-June, 1960

212

Solutions

No. 1 1 Qa5

In *Sam Loyd and his Chess Problems*, Alain White remarked: "I do not remember who the German critic was who first called Loyd's famous two-move Black interference scheme the Organ Pipes, but it was a very felicitous description." Loyd used this arrangement of black rooks and bishops in several problems. A rendering with a flight-square is shown in problem No. 21 by Wurzburg.

No. 2 1 Qd6

No. 3 1 Ba4

A problem by Carpenter, published the same month in the *Detroit Free Press*, was identical with No. 3, except that Carpenter's position had an unnecessary black pawn on e7. Such coincidences were not common then, as they have become since composers have made much more intensive studies of particular themes, and so this coincidence attracted far more attention than would the composing of identical positions today.

No. 4	1 Qf1	No. 5	1 Rf7	No. 6	1 Re1
No. 7	1 Qh5	No. 8	1 Qe1	No. 9	1 Qb4
No. 10	1 Qh5	No. 11	1 Rf7	No. 12	1 KRc2

Problems 11 and 12 won prizes in two different tourneys, both held in 1887 by the *Nashville American*.

No. 13	1 Qd2	No. 14	1 Sa3	No. 15	1 Qd2

No. 16 1 Ra6

This is an orthogonal version of the theme that Loyd dubbed the "American Indian," of which Loyd's earlier diagonal rendering is given in the note to problem 58. Actually the idea had been shown in orthogonal form as

early as 1885 by the eminent English composer B. G. La、
Another orthogonal rendering is Eaton's No. 119.   Hassber℧
achieves a miniature setting in No. 179.

B. G. Laws
The Morning Post
January 5, 1885

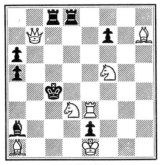

1 Re8

No. 17   1 Se6

The scheme of this composition has been shown in several
problems, and a prizewinner by Mackenzie antedates
Wurzburg's problem by some years.   Mackenzie, however,
used seventeen men to illustrate the idea, whereas Wurzburg
secures a far neater setting with only twelve.

A. F. Mackenzie
First Prize, ex æquo
Columbia Chess Chronicle
1888-1889

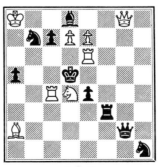

1 Sc6

No. 18	1 Pa4	No. 19	1 Ba1	No. 20	1 Q h7
No. 21	1 Rc1	No. 22	1 Q g4	No. 23	1 Be1
No. 24	1 Re1	No. 25	1 Qa4	No. 26	1 Q g1
No. 27	1 Kc4	No. 28	1 Rg3	No. 29	1 Rc4
No. 30	1 Be4				

The key subjects the bishop to capture by seven black men, with different mates in each case. Six of the captures result in self-blocks. Other composers who have illustrated this task have not been able to improve on the beauty of Marble's setting. An example by the Russian problemist Adabascheff has only fifteen men, but the flight-capture is initially set instead of being made possible by the key, as in Marble's masterpiece.

M. Adabascheff
The Western Morning News
November 9, 1935

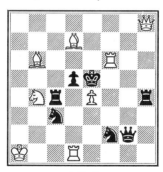

1 Be3

Six captures are shown in Sheppard's No. 200, in which black line openings are employed to differentiate the mates following three of the self-blocking captures.

No. 31   1 Pd3

This problem was composed specifically for the deceptive try, 1 Pd4. An en passant pawn capture by either black pawn opens a line for mate by the white queen, and an experienced solver, familiar with problems featuring such en passant captures, naturally might assume that 1 Pd4 was the key, with the threat of 2 Sb6 mate, especially in view of the set variation 1 — — Pf5 ck; 2 P × Pep, an en passant pawn capture by white. 1 Pd4, however, is defeated by 1 — — Bd8.

No. 31 suggested to the author the composition of No. 105, in which the try 1 Pc4 is met only by 1 — — Rb5.

No. 32 1 Rf4

No. 33 1 Pg7

This is a block-threat in which the key yields five flight-squares.

No. 34 1 Qc1

In this block-threat the unpinning of the black queen permits her to force five different mates.

No. 35 1 Qe1

No. 36 1 Rh4

It was in the two thematic variations of this problem that the term "Gamage theme" had its origin: 1 — — Pd6; 2 Qh8, and 1 — — Pd5; 2 Qh3.

As mentioned in the chapter on Strategic Elements, sometimes the Gamage theme and Przepiorka unpinning are spoken of as though they were identical. It might be useful, however, to make a distinction between the terms by applying the former where the interference of a black pawn on a line-pinned black queen permits her to be unpinned on the mating move, and using the latter where the unpinned black man is a rook, particularly where the interfering men are bishops or knights.

Gamage won an honorable mention in a tourney of the *Brisbane Courier* in 1915 with a problem which had three such interferences on a black rook, allowing the white queen to unpin the rook and deliver mate. The interferences were made respectively by a bishop, a knight and a pawn.

The following example shows five interferences on a rook, but the position is anticipated by a Meredith by J. Hartong, published in the *Good Companion Folder*, October, 1919 (No. 2288), which, however, had a flight-taking key.

Sándor Hertmann
Nationaltidende
1925

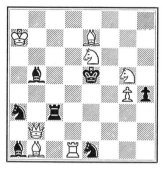

1 Ba2; threat 2 Rd5. 1 — — Bc4; 2 Qb8. 1 — — Bc6; 2 Qb8.
1 — — Sc4; Q × QB. 1 — — Bd3; 2 Qh2. 1 — — Sd3; 2 Qe2.

No. 37 1 Be2   No. 38 1 Bc3   No. 39 1 Qd2
No. 40 1 Q h4

This problem shows a doubled mutual pawn-Grimshaw interference. The four thematic variations are
1 — — Pd6; 2 Sc7: 1 — — Bd6; 2 Ba2: 1 — — Pf6;
2 R × Pe7: 1 — — Bf6; 2 Q × QB.

No. 41 1 Re6   No. 42 1 Kb3   No. 43 1 KRg5
No. 44 1 Qa3   No. 45 1 Qc3   No. 46 1 Rd8
No. 47 1 Rh6   No. 48 1 Sf4
No. 49 1 S × P

This problem illustrates what Frank Janet y-clept the
"Pickaninny theme," in which different mates follow each
of the four moves of a black pawn, that stands initially on the
seventh rank. This particular example is selected because
of its economical setting and the attractiveness of the mates.

No. 50 1 Se6   No. 51 1 Qd2   No. 52 1 R × BP
No. 53 1 Rg1   No. 54 1 Qb8   No. 55 1 KSd4
No. 56 1 Pe6   No. 57 1 Rb4

No. 58   1 Bf8

This position is a simplification of Loyd's intentionally rococo original diagonal setting of the American Indian theme, as shown in the accompanying diagram, with its mass of men that take no part in the play; reminiscent of the old practice of "dressing the board" to make a problem more gamelike in appearance.   Compare Kennard's rendering in No. 54.

Samuel Loyd
New York Sunday Herald
1889

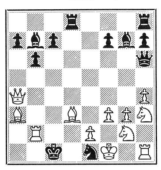

1 Bf 8

No. 59	1 Q g4	No. 60	1 Kc3	No. 61	1 Pc4
No. 62	1 Sa8	No. 63	1 Sf4	No. 64	1 Qb2
No. 65	1 Q S × P	No. 66	1 Sb6	No. 67	1 Pd4
No. 68	1 Qa1	No. 69	1 Qh7		
No. 70	1 Rc8				

J. Frank Stimson, born in Plainfield, New Jersey, in 1883, went to live on the island of Moörea, Society Islands, and on the occasion of his marriage was given the name Ua Tane, by Prince Hinoi Pomare of the Society Islands.

No. 71	1 Kg6	No. 72	1 Qe3	No. 73	1 Qe3
No. 74	1 Kc3	No. 75	1 Be3	No. 76	1 Qf5
No. 77	1 Qc7	No. 78	1 Pf4	No. 79	1 Rd7

No. 80   1 Qh4   No. 81   1 Rf4   No. 82   1 Sc3
No. 83   1 Qc4
No. 84   1 Qf6

The thematic try, 1 Qg6, with two different mates than those in the actual solution when the queen is unpinned, is defeated only by 1 —— Be4.

No. 85	1 Qg3	No. 86	1 Be5	No. 87	1 Qd4
No. 88	1 Bc1	No. 89	1 Rb8	No. 90	1 Pd4
No. 91	1 Pg6	No. 92	1 Sf6	No. 93	1 Bd5
No. 94	1 Qe5	No. 95	1 Qg7	No. 96	1 Q × P
No. 97	1 Qb7	No. 98	1 Qg1	No. 99	1 Kh2
No. 100	1 KSg6	No. 101	1 Rb8	No. 102	1 Qc7
No. 103	1 Sa5	No. 104	1 Bg7	No. 105	1 Pc3
No. 106	1 Qe7	No. 107	1 Re6	No. 108	1 Sg3
No. 109	1 Rc1	No. 110	1 Qg2	No. 111	1 Qe2
No. 112	1 KSb6	No. 113	1 Sd3	No. 114	1 Ke8
No. 115	1 Sd4	No. 116	1 Sd4	No. 117	1 Bh6
No. 118	1 Qe2	No. 119	1 Rb3	No. 120	1 Qd2
No. 121	1 Qc7	No. 122	1 Se4	No. 123	1 Bb4
No. 124	1 Bh5	No. 125	1 Bb1	No. 126	1 Qf3
No. 127	1 Qb1	No. 128	1 Qh3	No. 129	1 Sg2
No. 130	1 Bg8	No. 131	1 Sf4		
No. 132	1 Ke5				

It may be of interest to the solver to compare this problem with others in the collection where the king makes the key-move, viz., Nos. 42, 60, 71, 74, 99, 114, 136, 156, 159 and 197.

No. 133   1 Ra8   No. 134   1 Pd4
No. 135   1 Qb5

This problem was published after the composer's death, Kish having died on February 11, 1937.

No. 136	1 Ka2	No. 137	1 Rd6	No. 138	1 Qc1
No. 139	1 Sf7	No. 140	1 Re1	No. 141	1 Sd7
No. 142	1 Qa5	No. 143	1 Sd6	No. 144	1 Qb1

No. 145	1 Qf4	No. 146	1 Re7	No. 147	1 Bg3
No. 148	1 Qa1	No. 149	1 Qb1	No. 150	1 Rf4
No. 151	1 Bb6	No. 152	1 Qf4	No. 153	1 Qd4
No. 154	1 Sd2	No. 155	1 Sg6	No. 156	1 Kc4
No. 157	1 QSg2				
No. 158	1 Sa4				

This position is anticipated by a problem by the author, published November 13, 1926, in the *Brisbane Courier,* and rated as First Highly Commended in that newspaper's 22nd International Tourney.   No. 158 is slightly more economical and set more attractively than the author's rendering of the theme, which was reproduced as No. 44 in *The Enjoyment of Chess Problems.*   Also compare No. 35 by Gamage.

No. 159	1 Kc2	No. 160	1 Sh5	No. 161	1 Qf3
No. 162	1 Pd4	No. 163	1 Q g5		
No. 164	1 Rb3				

The tourney was restricted to problems with exactly ten men.

No. 165	1 Rf3	No. 166	1 Rb5	No. 167	1 Rc5
No. 168	1 Bg1	No. 169	1 Q g8	No. 170	1 Ba4
No. 171	1 Qe4	No. 172	1 Rc6	No. 173	1 Se3
No. 174	1 Rc5	No. 175	1 Pg7	No. 176	1 Sd3
No. 177	1 Bf6	No. 178	1 Se2	No. 179	1 Qc2
No. 180	1 Qa4				

This problem is anticipated by one by Dr. A. Chicco, published in *Il Problema,* September, 1934; but No. 180 has a more attractive and economical setting; with four fewer men than Dr. Chicco's rendering of the theme.

No. 181	1 Sf8	No. 182	1 Q × P	No. 183	1 Qc7
No. 184	1 Sc4	No. 185	1 Sd5	No. 186	1 Bh8
No. 187	1 Bc7	No. 188	1 Se1	No. 189	1 Pa6
No. 190	1 Sh4	No. 191	1 Sd5	No. 192	1 Bc1

No. 193	1 Sd4	No. 194	1 Bg3	No. 195	1 Qg8
No. 196	1 Qh4	No. 197	1 Kb6	No. 198	1 Qh4
No. 199	1 Qc6	No. 200	1 Se5	No. 201	1 Qg6
No. 202	1 Qf1	No. 203	1 Be4	No. 204	1 Qd8
No. 205	1 Qb3	No. 206	1 Bc4	No. 207	1 Q × Pc7
No. 208	1 Qf3	No. 209	1 Be3	No. 210	1 Re3
No. 211	1 Qe6	No. 212	1 Qc8		

Index of Composers

THE FIGURES REFER TO PROBLEM NUMBERS

General Index

THE FIGURES REFER TO PAGE NUMBERS

A CATALOGUE OF SELECTED DOVER BOOKS
IN ALL FIELDS OF INTEREST

A CATALOGUE OF SELECTED DOVER BOOKS
IN ALL FIELDS OF INTEREST

AMERICA'S OLD MASTERS, James T. Flexner. Four men emerged unexpectedly from provincial 18th century America to leadership in European art: Benjamin West, J. S. Copley, C. R. Peale, Gilbert Stuart. Brilliant coverage of lives and contributions. Revised, 1967 edition. 69 plates. 365pp. of text.

21806-6 Paperbound $3.00

FIRST FLOWERS OF OUR WILDERNESS: AMERICAN PAINTING, THE COLONIAL PERIOD, James T. Flexner. Painters, and regional painting traditions from earliest Colonial times up to the emergence of Copley, West and Peale Sr., Foster, Gustavus Hesselius, Feke, John Smibert and many anonymous painters in the primitive manner. Engaging presentation, with 162 illustrations. xxii + 368pp.

22180-6 Paperbound $3.50

THE LIGHT OF DISTANT SKIES: AMERICAN PAINTING, 1760-1835, James T. Flexner. The great generation of early American painters goes to Europe to learn and to teach: West, Copley, Gilbert Stuart and others. Allston, Trumbull, Morse; also contemporary American painters—primitives, derivatives, academics—who remained in America. 102 illustrations. xiii + 306pp.

22179-2 Paperbound $3.00

A HISTORY OF THE RISE AND PROGRESS OF THE ARTS OF DESIGN IN THE UNITED STATES, William Dunlap. Much the richest mine of information on early American painters, sculptors, architects, engravers, miniaturists, etc. The only source of information for scores of artists, the major primary source for many others. Unabridged reprint of rare original 1834 edition, with new introduction by James T. Flexner, and 394 new illustrations. Edited by Rita Weiss. 6⅝ x 9⅝.

21695-0, 21696-9, 21697-7 Three volumes, Paperbound $13.50

EPOCHS OF CHINESE AND JAPANESE ART, Ernest F. Fenollosa. From primitive Chinese art to the 20th century, thorough history, explanation of every important art period and form, including Japanese woodcuts; main stress on China and Japan, but Tibet, Korea also included. Still unexcelled for its detailed, rich coverage of cultural background, aesthetic elements, diffusion studies, particularly of the historical period. 2nd, 1913 edition. 242 illustrations. lii + 439pp. of text.

20364-6, 20365-4 Two volumes, Paperbound $6.00

THE GENTLE ART OF MAKING ENEMIES, James A. M. Whistler. Greatest wit of his day deflates Oscar Wilde, Ruskin, Swinburne; strikes back at inane critics, exhibitions, art journalism; aesthetics of impressionist revolution in most striking form. Highly readable classic by great painter. Reproduction of edition designed by Whistler. Introduction by Alfred Werner. xxxvi + 334pp.

21875-9 Paperbound $2.50

VISUAL ILLUSIONS: THEIR CAUSES, CHARACTERISTICS, AND APPLICATIONS, Matthew Luckiesh. Thorough description and discussion of optical illusion, geometric and perspective, particularly; size and shape distortions, illusions of color, of motion; natural illusions; use of illusion in art and magic, industry, etc. Most useful today with op art, also for classical art. Scores of effects illustrated. Introduction by William H. Ittleson. 100 illustrations. xxi + 252pp.

21530-X Paperbound $2.00

A HANDBOOK OF ANATOMY FOR ART STUDENTS, Arthur Thomson. Thorough, virtually exhaustive coverage of skeletal structure, musculature, etc. Full text, supplemented by anatomical diagrams and drawings and by photographs of undraped figures. Unique in its comparison of male and female forms, pointing out differences of contour, texture, form. 211 figures, 40 drawings, 86 photographs. xx + 459pp. 5⅜ x 8⅜.

21163-0 Paperbound $3.50

150 MASTERPIECES OF DRAWING, Selected by Anthony Toney. Full page reproductions of drawings from the early 16th to the end of the 18th century, all beautifully reproduced: Rembrandt, Michelangelo, Dürer, Fragonard, Urs, Graf, Wouwerman, many others. First-rate browsing book, model book for artists. xviii + 150pp. 8⅜ x 11¼.

21032-4 Paperbound $2.50

THE LATER WORK OF AUBREY BEARDSLEY, Aubrey Beardsley. Exotic, erotic, ironic masterpieces in full maturity: Comedy Ballet, Venus and Tannhauser, Pierrot, Lysistrata, Rape of the Lock, Savoy material, Ali Baba, Volpone, etc. This material revolutionized the art world, and is still powerful, fresh, brilliant. With *The Early Work*, all Beardsley's finest work. 174 plates, 2 in color. xiv + 176pp. 8⅛ x 11.

21817-1 Paperbound $3.00

DRAWINGS OF REMBRANDT, Rembrandt van Rijn. Complete reproduction of fabulously rare edition by Lippmann and Hofstede de Groot, completely reedited, updated, improved by Prof. Seymour Slive, Fogg Museum. Portraits, Biblical sketches, landscapes, Oriental types, nudes, episodes from classical mythology—All Rembrandt's fertile genius. Also selection of drawings by his pupils and followers. "Stunning volumes," *Saturday Review.* 550 illustrations. lxxviii + 552pp. 9⅛ x 12¼.

21485-0, 21486-9 Two volumes, Paperbound $10.00

THE DISASTERS OF WAR, Francisco Goya. One of the masterpieces of Western civilization—83 etchings that record Goya's shattering, bitter reaction to the Napoleonic war that swept through Spain after the insurrection of 1808 and to war in general. Reprint of the first edition, with three additional plates from Boston's Museum of Fine Arts. All plates facsimile size. Introduction by Philip Hofer, Fogg Museum. v + 97pp. 9⅜ x 8¼.

21872-4 Paperbound $2.00

GRAPHIC WORKS OF ODILON REDON. Largest collection of Redon's graphic works ever assembled: 172 lithographs, 28 etchings and engravings, 9 drawings. These include some of his most famous works. All the plates from *Odilon Redon: oeuvre graphique complet,* plus additional plates. New introduction and caption translations by Alfred Werner. 209 illustrations. xxvii + 209pp. 9⅛ x 12¼.

21966-8 Paperbound $4.00

DESIGN BY ACCIDENT; A BOOK OF "ACCIDENTAL EFFECTS" FOR ARTISTS AND DESIGNERS, James F. O'Brien. Create your own unique, striking, imaginative effects by "controlled accident" interaction of materials: paints and lacquers, oil and water based paints, splatter, crackling materials, shatter, similar items. Everything you do will be different; first book on this limitless art, so useful to both fine artist and commercial artist. Full instructions. 192 plates showing "accidents," 8 in color. viii + 215pp. 8⅜ x 11¼. 21942-9 Paperbound $3.50

THE BOOK OF SIGNS, Rudolf Koch. Famed German type designer draws 493 beautiful symbols: religious, mystical, alchemical, imperial, property marks, runes, etc. Remarkable fusion of traditional and modern. Good for suggestions of timelessness, smartness, modernity. Text. vi + 104pp. 6⅛ x 9¼.
20162-7 Paperbound $1.25

HISTORY OF INDIAN AND INDONESIAN ART, Ananda K. Coomaraswamy. An unabridged republication of one of the finest books by a great scholar in Eastern art. Rich in descriptive material, history, social backgrounds; Sunga reliefs, Rajput paintings, Gupta temples, Burmese frescoes, textiles, jewelry, sculpture, etc. 400 photos. viii + 423pp. 6⅜ x 9¾. 21436-2 Paperbound $4.00

PRIMITIVE ART, Franz Boas. America's foremost anthropologist surveys textiles, ceramics, woodcarving, basketry, metalwork, etc.; patterns, technology, creation of symbols, style origins. All areas of world, but very full on Northwest Coast Indians. More than 350 illustrations of baskets, boxes, totem poles, weapons, etc. 378 pp.
20025-6 Paperbound $3.00

THE GENTLEMAN AND CABINET MAKER'S DIRECTOR, Thomas Chippendale. Full reprint (third edition, 1762) of most influential furniture book of all time, by master cabinetmaker. 200 plates, illustrating chairs, sofas, mirrors, tables, cabinets, plus 24 photographs of surviving pieces. Biographical introduction by N. Bienenstock. vi + 249pp. 9⅞ x 12¾. 21601-2 Paperbound $4.00

AMERICAN ANTIQUE FURNITURE, Edgar G. Miller, Jr. The basic coverage of all American furniture before 1840. Individual chapters cover type of furniture— clocks, tables, sideboards, etc.—chronologically, with inexhaustible wealth of data. More than 2100 photographs, all identified, commented on. Essential to all early American collectors. Introduction by H. E. Keyes. vi + 1106pp. 7⅞ x 10¾.
21599-7, 21600-4 Two volumes, Paperbound $11.00

PENNSYLVANIA DUTCH AMERICAN FOLK ART, Henry J. Kauffman. 279 photos, 28 drawings of tulipware, Fraktur script, painted tinware, toys, flowered furniture, quilts, samplers, hex signs, house interiors, etc. Full descriptive text. Excellent for tourist, rewarding for designer, collector. Map. 146pp. 7⅞ x 10¾.
21205-X Paperbound $2.50

EARLY NEW ENGLAND GRAVESTONE RUBBINGS, Edmund V. Gillon, Jr. 43 photographs, 226 carefully reproduced rubbings show heavily symbolic, sometimes macabre early gravestones, up to early 19th century. Remarkable early American primitive art, occasionally strikingly beautiful; always powerful. Text. xxvi + 207pp. 8⅜ x 11¼. 21380-3 Paperbound $3.50

ALPHABETS AND ORNAMENTS, Ernst Lehner. Well-known pictorial source for decorative alphabets, script examples, cartouches, frames, decorative title pages, calligraphic initials, borders, similar material. 14th to 19th century, mostly European. Useful in almost any graphic arts designing, varied styles. 750 illustrations. 256pp. 7 x 10. 21905-4 Paperbound $4.00

PAINTING: A CREATIVE APPROACH, Norman Colquhoun. For the beginner simple guide provides an instructive approach to painting: major stumbling blocks for beginner; overcoming them, technical points; paints and pigments; oil painting; watercolor and other media and color. New section on "plastic" paints. Glossary. Formerly *Paint Your Own Pictures*. 221pp. 22000-1 Paperbound $1.75

THE ENJOYMENT AND USE OF COLOR, Walter Sargent. Explanation of the relations between colors themselves and between colors in nature and art, including hundreds of little-known facts about color values, intensities, effects of high and low illumination, complementary colors. Many practical hints for painters, references to great masters. 7 color plates, 29 illustrations. x + 274pp.
20944-X Paperbound $2.75

THE NOTEBOOKS OF LEONARDO DA VINCI, compiled and edited by Jean Paul Richter. 1566 extracts from original manuscripts reveal the full range of Leonardo's versatile genius: all his writings on painting, sculpture, architecture, anatomy, astronomy, geography, topography, physiology, mining, music, etc., in both Italian and English, with 186 plates of manuscript pages and more than 500 additional drawings. Includes studies for the Last Supper, the lost Sforza monument, and other works. Total of xlvii + 866pp. 7⅞ x 10¾.
22572-0, 22573-9 Two volumes, Paperbound $10.00

MONTGOMERY WARD CATALOGUE OF 1895. Tea gowns, yards of flannel and pillow-case lace, stereoscopes, books of gospel hymns, the New Improved Singer Sewing Machine, side saddles, milk skimmers, straight-edged razors, high-button shoes, spittoons, and on and on . . . listing some 25,000 items, practically all illustrated. Essential to the shoppers of the 1890's, it is our truest record of the spirit of the period. Unaltered reprint of Issue No. 57, Spring and Summer 1895. Introduction by Boris Emmet. Innumerable illustrations. xiii + 624pp. 8½ x 11⅝.
22377-9 Paperbound $6.95

THE CRYSTAL PALACE EXHIBITION ILLUSTRATED CATALOGUE (LONDON, 1851). One of the wonders of the modern world—the Crystal Palace Exhibition in which all the nations of the civilized world exhibited their achievements in the arts and sciences—presented in an equally important illustrated catalogue. More than 1700 items pictured with accompanying text—ceramics, textiles, cast-iron work, carpets, pianos, sleds, razors, wall-papers, billiard tables, beehives, silverware and hundreds of other artifacts—represent the focal point of Victorian culture in the Western World. Probably the largest collection of Victorian decorative art ever assembled—indispensable for antiquarians and designers. Unabridged republication of the Art-Journal Catalogue of the Great Exhibition of 1851, with all terminal essays. New introduction by John Gloag, F.S.A. xxxiv + 426pp. 9 x 12.
22503-8 Paperbound $4.50

A History of Costume, Carl Köhler. Definitive history, based on surviving pieces of clothing primarily, and paintings, statues, etc. secondarily. Highly readable text, supplemented by 594 illustrations of costumes of the ancient Mediterranean peoples, Greece and Rome, the Teutonic prehistoric period; costumes of the Middle Ages, Renaissance, Baroque, 18th and 19th centuries. Clear, measured patterns are provided for many clothing articles. Approach is practical throughout. Enlarged by Emma von Sichart. 464pp.   21030-8 Paperbound $3.50

Oriental Rugs, Antique and Modern, Walter A. Hawley. A complete and authoritative treatise on the Oriental rug—where they are made, by whom and how, designs and symbols, characteristics in detail of the six major groups, how to distinguish them and how to buy them. Detailed technical data is provided on periods, weaves, warps, wefts, textures, sides, ends and knots, although no technical background is required for an understanding. 11 color plates, 80 halftones, 4 maps. vi + 320pp. 6⅛ x 9⅛.   22366-3 Paperbound $5.00

Ten Books on Architecture, Vitruvius. By any standards the most important book on architecture ever written. Early Roman discussion of aesthetics of building, construction methods, orders, sites, and every other aspect of architecture has inspired, instructed architecture for about 2,000 years. Stands behind Palladio, Michelangelo, Bramante, Wren, countless others. Definitive Morris H. Morgan translation. 68 illustrations. xii + 331pp.   20645-9 Paperbound $3.50

The Four Books of Architecture, Andrea Palladio. Translated into every major Western European language in the two centuries following its publication in 1570, this has been one of the most influential books in the history of architecture. Complete reprint of the 1738 Isaac Ware edition. New introduction by Adolf Placzek, Columbia Univ. 216 plates. xxii + 110pp. of text. 9½ x 12¾.
21308-0 Clothbound $10.00

Sticks and Stones: A Study of American Architecture and Civilization, Lewis Mumford. One of the great classics of American cultural history. American architecture from the medieval-inspired earliest forms to the early 20th century; evolution of structure and style, and reciprocal influences on environment. 21 photographic illustrations. 238pp.   20202-X Paperbound $2.00

The American Builder's Companion, Asher Benjamin. The most widely used early 19th century architectural style and source book, for colonial up into Greek Revival periods. Extensive development of geometry of carpentering, construction of sashes, frames, doors, stairs; plans and elevations of domestic and other buildings. Hundreds of thousands of houses were built according to this book, now invaluable to historians, architects, restorers, etc. 1827 edition. 59 plates. 114pp. 7⅞ x 10¾.
22236-5 Paperbound $3.50

Dutch Houses in the Hudson Valley Before 1776, Helen Wilkinson Reynolds. The standard survey of the Dutch colonial house and outbuildings, with constructional features, decoration, and local history associated with individual homesteads. Introduction by Franklin D. Roosevelt. Map. 150 illustrations. 469pp. 6⅝ x 9¼.   21469-9 Paperbound $4.00

THE ARCHITECTURE OF COUNTRY HOUSES, Andrew J. Downing. Together with Vaux's *Villas and Cottages* this is the basic book for Hudson River Gothic architecture of the middle Victorian period. Full, sound discussions of general aspects of housing, architecture, style, decoration, furnishing, together with scores of detailed house plans, illustrations of specific buildings, accompanied by full text. Perhaps the most influential single American architectural book. 1850 edition. Introduction by J. Stewart Johnson. 321 figures, 34 architectural designs. xvi + 560pp.
22003-6 Paperbound $4.00

LOST EXAMPLES OF COLONIAL ARCHITECTURE, John Mead Howells. Full-page photographs of buildings that have disappeared or been so altered as to be denatured, including many designed by major early American architects. 245 plates. xvii + 248pp. 7⅞ x 10¾. 21143-6 Paperbound $3.50

DOMESTIC ARCHITECTURE OF THE AMERICAN COLONIES AND OF THE EARLY REPUBLIC, Fiske Kimball. Foremost architect and restorer of Williamsburg and Monticello covers nearly 200 homes between 1620-1825. Architectural details, construction, style features, special fixtures, floor plans, etc. Generally considered finest work in its area. 219 illustrations of houses, doorways, windows, capital mantels. xx + 314pp. 7⅞ x 10¾. 21743-4 Paperbound $4.00

EARLY AMERICAN ROOMS: 1650-1858, edited by Russell Hawes Kettell. Tour of 12 rooms, each representative of a different era in American history and each furnished, decorated, designed and occupied in the style of the era. 72 plans and elevations, 8-page color section, etc., show fabrics, wall papers, arrangements, etc. Full descriptive text. xvii + 200pp. of text. 8⅜ x 11¼.
21633-0 Paperbound $5.00

THE FITZWILLIAM VIRGINAL BOOK, edited by J. Fuller Maitland and W. B. Squire. Full modern printing of famous early 17th-century ms. volume of 300 works by Morley, Byrd, Bull, Gibbons, etc. For piano or other modern keyboard instrument; easy to read format. xxxvi + 938pp. 8⅜ x 11.
21068-5, 21069-3 Two volumes, Paperbound $10.00

KEYBOARD MUSIC, Johann Sebastian Bach. Bach Gesellschaft edition. A rich selection of Bach's masterpieces for the harpsichord: the six English Suites, six French Suites, the six Partitas (Clavierübung part I), the Goldberg Variations (Clavierübung part IV), the fifteen Two-Part Inventions and the fifteen Three-Part Sinfonias. Clearly reproduced on large sheets with ample margins; eminently playable. vi + 312pp. 8⅛ x 11. 22360-4 Paperbound $5.00

THE MUSIC OF BACH: AN INTRODUCTION, Charles Sanford Terry. A fine, nontechnical introduction to Bach's music, both instrumental and vocal. Covers organ music, chamber music, passion music, other types. Analyzes themes, developments, innovations. x + 114pp. 21075-8 Paperbound $1.25

BEETHOVEN AND HIS NINE SYMPHONIES, Sir George Grove. Noted British musicologist provides best history, analysis, commentary on symphonies. Very thorough, rigorously accurate; necessary to both advanced student and amateur music lover. 436 musical passages. vii + 407 pp. 20334-4 Paperbound $2.75

JOHANN SEBASTIAN BACH, Philipp Spitta. One of the great classics of musicology, this definitive analysis of Bach's music (and life) has never been surpassed. Lucid, nontechnical analyses of hundreds of pieces (30 pages devoted to St. Matthew Passion, 26 to B Minor Mass). Also includes major analysis of 18th-century music. 450 musical examples. 40-page musical supplement. Total of xx + 1799pp.
(EUK) 22278-0, 22279-9 Two volumes, Clothbound $17.50

MOZART AND HIS PIANO CONCERTOS, Cuthbert Girdlestone. The only full-length study of an important area of Mozart's creativity. Provides detailed analyses of all 23 concertos, traces inspirational sources. 417 musical examples. Second edition. 509pp.   (USO) 21271-8 Paperbound $3.50

THE PERFECT WAGNERITE: A COMMENTARY ON THE NIBLUNG'S RING, George Bernard Shaw. Brilliant and ˙still relevant criticism in remarkable essays on Wagner's Ring cycle, Shaw's ideas on political and social ideology behind the plots, role of Leitmotifs, vocal requisites, etc. Prefaces. xxi + 136pp.
21707-8 Paperbound $1.50

DON GIOVANNI, W. A. Mozart. Complete libretto, modern English translation; biographies of composer and librettist; accounts of early performances and critical reaction. Lavishly illustrated. All the material you need to understand and appreciate this great work. Dover Opera Guide and Libretto Series; translated and introduced by Ellen Bleiler. 92 illustrations. 209pp.
21134-7 Paperbound $2.00

HIGH FIDELITY SYSTEMS: A LAYMAN'S GUIDE, Roy F. Allison. All the basic information you need for setting up your own audio system: high fidelity and stereo record players, tape records, F.M. Connections, adjusting tone arm, cartridge, checking needle alignment, positioning speakers, phasing speakers, adjusting hums, trouble-shooting, maintenance, and similar topics. Enlarged 1965 edition. More than 50 charts, diagrams, photos. iv + 91pp.   21514-8 Paperbound $1.25

REPRODUCTION OF SOUND, Edgar Villchur. Thorough coverage for laymen of high fidelity systems, reproducing systems in general, needles, amplifiers, preamps, loudspeakers, feedback, explaining physical background. "A rare talent for making technicalities vividly comprehensible," R. Darrell, *High Fidelity*. 69 figures. iv + 92pp.   21515-6 Paperbound $1.25

HEAR ME TALKIN' TO YA: THE STORY OF JAZZ AS TOLD BY THE MEN WHO MADE IT, Nat Shapiro and Nat Hentoff. Louis Armstrong, Fats Waller, Jo Jones, Clarence Williams, Billy Holiday, Duke Ellington, Jelly Roll Morton and dozens of other jazz greats tell how it was in Chicago's South Side, New Orleans, depression Harlem and the modern West Coast as jazz was born and grew. xvi + 429pp.
21726-4 Paperbound $2.50

FABLES OF AESOP, translated by Sir Roger L'Estrange. A reproduction of the very rare 1931 Paris edition; a selection of the most interesting fables, together with 50 imaginative drawings by Alexander Calder. v + 128pp. 6½x9¼.
21780-9 Paperbound ˙$1.50

AGAINST THE GRAIN (A REBOURS), Joris K. Huysmans. Filled with weird images, evidences of a bizarre imagination, exotic experiments with hallucinatory drugs, rich tastes and smells and the diversions of its sybarite hero Duc Jean des Esseintes, this classic novel pushed 19th-century literary decadence to its limits. Full unabridged edition. Do not confuse this with abridged editions generally sold. Introduction by Havelock Ellis. xlix + 206pp.   22190-3 Paperbound $2.00

VARIORUM SHAKESPEARE: HAMLET. Edited by Horace H. Furness; a landmark of American scholarship. Exhaustive footnotes and appendices treat all doubtful words and phrases, as well as suggested critical emendations throughout the play's history. First volume contains editor's own text, collated with all Quartos and Folios. Second volume contains full first Quarto, translations of Shakespeare's sources (Belleforest, and Saxo Grammaticus), Der Bestrafte Brudermord, and many essays on critical and historical points of interest by major authorities of past and present. Includes details of staging and costuming over the years. By far the best edition available for serious students of Shakespeare. Total of xx + 905pp.
21004-9, 21005-7, 2 volumes, Paperbound $7.00

A LIFE OF WILLIAM SHAKESPEARE, Sir Sidney Lee. This is the standard life of Shakespeare, summarizing everything known about Shakespeare and his plays. Incredibly rich in material, broad in coverage, clear and judicious, it has served thousands as the best introduction to Shakespeare. 1931 edition. 9 plates. xxix + 792pp.   (USO) 21967-4 Paperbound $3.75

MASTERS OF THE DRAMA, John Gassner. Most comprehensive history of the drama in print, covering every tradition from Greeks to modern Europe and America, including India, Far East, etc. Covers more than 800 dramatists, 2000 plays, with biographical material, plot summaries, theatre history, criticism, etc. "Best of its kind in English," New Republic. 77 illustrations. xxii + 890pp.
20100-7 Clothbound $8.50

THE EVOLUTION OF THE ENGLISH LANGUAGE, George McKnight. The growth of English, from the 14th century to the present. Unusual, non-technical account presents basic information in very interesting form: sound shifts, change in grammar and syntax, vocabulary growth, similar topics. Abundantly illustrated with quotations. Formerly Modern English in the Making. xii + 590pp.
21932-1 Paperbound $3.50

AN ETYMOLOGICAL DICTIONARY OF MODERN ENGLISH, Ernest Weekley. Fullest, richest work of its sort, by foremost British lexicographer. Detailed word histories, including many colloquial and archaic words; extensive quotations. Do not confuse this with the Concise Etymological Dictionary, which is much abridged. Total of xxvii + 830pp. 6½ x 9¼.
21873-2, 21874-0 Two volumes, Paperbound $6.00

FLATLAND: A ROMANCE OF MANY DIMENSIONS, E. A. Abbott. Classic of science-fiction explores ramifications of life in a two-dimensional world, and what happens when a three-dimensional being intrudes. Amusing reading, but also useful as introduction to thought about hyperspace. Introduction by Banesh Hoffmann. 16 illustrations. xx + 103pp.   20001-9 Paperbound $1.00

POEMS OF ANNE BRADSTREET, edited with an introduction by Robert Hutchinson. A new selection of poems by America's first poet and perhaps the first significant woman poet in the English language. 48 poems display her development in works of considerable variety—love poems, domestic poems, religious meditations, formal elegies, "quaternions," etc. Notes, bibliography. viii + 222pp.
22160-1 Paperbound $2.00

THREE GOTHIC NOVELS: THE CASTLE OF OTRANTO BY HORACE WALPOLE; VATHEK BY WILLIAM BECKFORD; THE VAMPYRE BY JOHN POLIDORI, WITH FRAGMENT OF A NOVEL BY LORD BYRON, edited by E. F. Bleiler. The first Gothic novel, by Walpole; the finest Oriental tale in English, by Beckford; powerful Romantic supernatural story in versions by Polidori and Byron. All extremely important in history of literature; all still exciting, packed with supernatural thrills, ghosts, haunted castles, magic, etc. xl + 291pp.
21232-7 Paperbound $2.50

THE BEST TALES OF HOFFMANN, E. T. A. Hoffmann. 10 of Hoffmann's most important stories, in modern re-editings of standard translations: Nutcracker and the King of Mice, Signor Formica, Automata, The Sandman, Rath Krespel, The Golden Flowerpot, Master Martin the Cooper, The Mines of Falun, The King's Betrothed, A New Year's Eve Adventure. 7 illustrations by Hoffmann. Edited by E. F. Bleiler. xxxix + 419pp.
21793-0 Paperbound $3.00

GHOST AND HORROR STORIES OF AMBROSE BIERCE, Ambrose Bierce. 23 strikingly modern stories of the horrors latent in the human mind: The Eyes of the Panther, The Damned Thing, An Occurrence at Owl Creek Bridge, An Inhabitant of Carcosa, etc., plus the dream-essay, Visions of the Night. Edited by E. F. Bleiler. xxii + 199pp.
20767-6 Paperbound $1.50

BEST GHOST STORIES OF J. S. LeFANU, J. Sheridan LeFanu. Finest stories by Victorian master often considered greatest supernatural writer of all. Carmilla, Green Tea, The Haunted Baronet, The Familiar, and 12 others. Most never before available in the U. S. A. Edited by E. F. Bleiler. 8 illustrations from Victorian publications. xvii + 467pp.
20415-4 Paperbound $3.00

MATHEMATICAL FOUNDATIONS OF INFORMATION THEORY, A. I. Khinchin. Comprehensive introduction to work of Shannon, McMillan, Feinstein and Khinchin, placing these investigations on a rigorous mathematical basis. Covers entropy concept in probability theory, uniqueness theorem, Shannon's inequality, ergodic sources, the E property, martingale concept, noise, Feinstein's fundamental lemma, Shanon's first and second theorems. Translated by R. A. Silverman and M. D. Friedman. iii + 120pp.
60434-9 Paperbound $1.75

SEVEN SCIENCE FICTION NOVELS, H. G. Wells. The standard collection of the great novels. Complete, unabridged. *First Men in the Moon, Island of Dr. Moreau, War of the Worlds, Food of the Gods, Invisible Man, Time Machine, In the Days of the Comet.* Not only science fiction fans, but every educated person owes it to himself to read these novels. 1015pp.
20264-X Clothbound $5.00

LAST AND FIRST MEN AND STAR MAKER, TWO SCIENCE FICTION NOVELS, Olaf Stapledon. Greatest future histories in science fiction. In the first, human intelligence is the "hero," through strange paths of evolution, interplanetary invasions, incredible technologies, near extinctions and reemergences. Star Maker describes the quest of a band of star rovers for intelligence itself, through time and space: weird inhuman civilizations, crustacean minds, symbiotic worlds, etc. Complete, unabridged. v + 438pp. 21962-3 Paperbound $2.50

THREE PROPHETIC NOVELS, H. G. WELLS. Stages of a consistently planned future for mankind. *When the Sleeper Wakes,* and *A Story of the Days to Come,* anticipate *Brave New World* and *1984,* in the 21st Century; *The Time Machine,* only complete version in print, shows farther future and the end of mankind. All show Wells's greatest gifts as storyteller and novelist. Edited by E. F. Bleiler. x + 335pp. (USO) 20605-X Paperbound $2.50

THE DEVIL'S DICTIONARY, Ambrose Bierce. America's own Oscar Wilde—Ambrose Bierce—offers his barbed iconoclastic wisdom in over 1,000 definitions hailed by H. L. Mencken as "some of the most gorgeous witticisms in the English language." 145pp. 20487-1 Paperbound $1.25

MAX AND MORITZ, Wilhelm Busch. Great children's classic, father of comic strip, of two bad boys, Max and Moritz. Also Ker and Plunk (Plisch und Plumm), Cat and Mouse, Deceitful Henry, Ice-Peter, The Boy and the Pipe, and five other pieces. Original German, with English translation. Edited by H. Arthur Klein; translations by various hands and H. Arthur Klein. vi + 216pp.
20181-3 Paperbound $2.00

PIGS IS PIGS AND OTHER FAVORITES, Ellis Parker Butler. The title story is one of the best humor short stories, as Mike Flannery obfuscates biology and English. Also included, That Pup of Murchison's, The Great American Pie Company, and Perkins of Portland. 14 illustrations. v + 109pp. 21532-6 Paperbound $1.25

THE PETERKIN PAPERS, Lucretia P. Hale. It takes genius to be as stupidly mad as the Peterkins, as they decide to become wise, celebrate the "Fourth," keep a cow, and otherwise strain the resources of the Lady from Philadelphia. Basic book of American humor. 153 illustrations. 219pp. 20794-3 Paperbound $1.50

PERRAULT'S FAIRY TALES, translated by A. E. Johnson and S. R. Littlewood, with 34 full-page illustrations by Gustave Doré. All the original Perrault stories—Cinderella, Sleeping Beauty, Bluebeard, Little Red Riding Hood, Puss in Boots, Tom Thumb, etc.—with their witty verse morals and the magnificent illustrations of Doré. One of the five or six great books of European fairy tales. viii + 117pp. 8⅛ x 11. 22311-6 Paperbound $2.00

OLD HUNGARIAN FAIRY TALES, Baroness Orczy. Favorites translated and adapted by author of the *Scarlet Pimpernel.* Eight fairy tales include "The Suitors of Princess Fire-Fly," "The Twin Hunchbacks," "Mr. Cuttlefish's Love Story," and "The Enchanted Cat." This little volume of magic and adventure will captivate children as it has for generations. 90 drawings by Montagu Barstow. 96pp.
(USO) 22293-4 Paperbound $1.95

THE RED FAIRY BOOK, Andrew Lang. Lang's color fairy books have long been children's favorites. This volume includes Rapunzel, Jack and the Bean-stalk and 35 other stories, familiar and unfamiliar. 4 plates, 93 illustrations x + 367pp.
21673-X Paperbound $2.50

THE BLUE FAIRY BOOK, Andrew Lang. Lang's tales come from all countries and all times. Here are 37 tales from Grimm, the Arabian Nights, Greek Mythology, and other fascinating sources. 8 plates, 130 illustrations. xi + 390pp.
21437-0 Paperbound $2.50

HOUSEHOLD STORIES BY THE BROTHERS GRIMM. Classic English-language edition of the well-known tales — Rumpelstiltskin, Snow White, Hansel and Gretel, The Twelve Brothers, Faithful John, Rapunzel, Tom Thumb (52 stories in all). Translated into simple, straightforward English by Lucy Crane. Ornamented with headpieces, vignettes, elaborate decorative initials and a dozen full-page illustrations by Walter Crane. x + 269pp.
21080-4 Paperbound $2.50

THE MERRY ADVENTURES OF ROBIN HOOD, Howard Pyle. The finest modern versions of the traditional ballads and tales about the great English outlaw. Howard Pyle's complete prose version, with every word, every illustration of the first edition. Do not confuse this facsimile of the original (1883) with modern editions that change text or illustrations. 23 plates plus many page decorations. xxii + 296pp.
22043-5 Paperbound $2.50

THE STORY OF KING ARTHUR AND HIS KNIGHTS, Howard Pyle. The finest children's version of the life of King Arthur; brilliantly retold by Pyle, with 48 of his most imaginative illustrations. xviii + 313pp. 6⅛ x 9¼.
21445-1 Paperbound $2.50

THE WONDERFUL WIZARD OF OZ, L. Frank Baum. America's finest children's book in facsimile of first edition with all Denslow illustrations in full color. The edition a child should have. Introduction by Martin Gardner. 23 color plates, scores of drawings. iv + 267pp.
20691-2 Paperbound $2.50

THE MARVELOUS LAND OF OZ, L. Frank Baum. The second Oz book, every bit as imaginative as the Wizard. The hero is a boy named Tip, but the Scarecrow and the Tin Woodman are back, as is the Oz magic. 16 color plates, 120 drawings by John R. Neill. 287pp.
20692-0 Paperbound $2.50

THE MAGICAL MONARCH OF MO, L. Frank Baum. Remarkable adventures in a land even stranger than Oz. The best of Baum's books not in the Oz series. 15 color plates and dozens of drawings by Frank Verbeck. xviii + 237pp.
21892-9 Paperbound $2.25

THE BAD CHILD'S BOOK OF BEASTS, MORE BEASTS FOR WORSE CHILDREN, A MORAL ALPHABET, Hilaire Belloc. Three complete humor classics in one volume. Be kind to the frog, and do not call him names . . . and 28 other whimsical animals. Familiar favorites and some not so well known. Illustrated by Basil Blackwell. 156pp.
(USO) 20749-8 Paperbound $1.50

EAST O' THE SUN AND WEST O' THE MOON, George W. Dasent. Considered the best of all translations of these Norwegian folk tales, this collection has been enjoyed by generations of children (and folklorists too). Includes True and Untrue, Why the Sea is Salt, East O' the Sun and West O' the Moon, Why the Bear is Stumpy-Tailed, Boots and the Troll, The Cock and the Hen, Rich Peter the Pedlar, and 52 more. The only edition with all 59 tales. 77 illustrations by Erik Werenskiold and Theodor Kittelsen. xv + 418pp. 22521-6 Paperbound $3.50

GOOPS AND HOW TO BE THEM, Gelett Burgess. Classic of tongue-in-cheek humor, masquerading as etiquette book. 87 verses, twice as many cartoons, show mischievous Goops as they demonstrate to children virtues of table manners, neatness, courtesy, etc. Favorite for generations. viii + 88pp. 6½ x 9¼.
22233-0 Paperbound $1.25

ALICE'S ADVENTURES UNDER GROUND, Lewis Carroll. The first version, quite different from the final *Alice in Wonderland,* printed out by Carroll himself with his own illustrations. Complete facsimile of the "million dollar" manuscript Carroll gave to Alice Liddell in 1864. Introduction by Martin Gardner. viii + 96pp. Title and dedication pages in color. 21482-6 Paperbound $1.25

THE BROWNIES, THEIR BOOK, Palmer Cox. Small as mice, cunning as foxes, exuberant and full of mischief, the Brownies go to the zoo, toy shop, seashore, circus, etc., in 24 verse adventures and 266 illustrations. Long a favorite, since their first appearance in St. Nicholas Magazine. xi + 144pp. 6⅝ x 9¼.
21265-3 Paperbound $1.75

SONGS OF CHILDHOOD, Walter De La Mare. Published (under the pseudonym Walter Ramal) when De La Mare was only 29, this charming collection has long been a favorite children's book. A facsimile of the first edition in paper, the 47 poems capture the simplicity of the nursery rhyme and the ballad, including such lyrics as I Met Eve, Tartary, The Silver Penny. vii + 106pp. 21972-0 Paperbound $1.25

THE COMPLETE NONSENSE OF EDWARD LEAR, Edward Lear. The finest 19th-century humorist-cartoonist in full: all nonsense limericks, zany alphabets, Owl and Pussycat, songs, nonsense botany, and more than 500 illustrations by Lear himself. Edited by Holbrook Jackson. xxix + 287pp. (USO) 20167-8 Paperbound $2.00

BILLY WHISKERS: THE AUTOBIOGRAPHY OF A GOAT, Frances Trego Montgomery. A favorite of children since the early 20th century, here are the escapades of that rambunctious, irresistible and mischievous goat—Billy Whiskers. Much in the spirit of *Peck's Bad Boy,* this is a book that children never tire of reading or hearing. All the original familiar illustrations by W. H. Fry are included: 6 color plates, 18 black and white drawings. 159pp. 22345-0 Paperbound $2.00

MOTHER GOOSE MELODIES. Faithful republication of the fabulously rare Munroe and Francis "copyright 1833" Boston edition—the most important Mother Goose collection, usually referred to as the "original." Familiar rhymes plus many rare ones, with wonderful old woodcut illustrations. Edited by E. F. Bleiler. 128pp. 4½ x 6⅜. 22577-1 Paperbound $1.25

TWO LITTLE SAVAGES; BEING THE ADVENTURES OF TWO BOYS WHO LIVED AS INDIANS AND WHAT THEY LEARNED, Ernest Thompson Seton. Great classic of nature and boyhood provides a vast range of woodlore in most palatable form, a genuinely entertaining story. Two farm boys build a teepee in woods and live in it for a month, working out Indian solutions to living problems, star lore, birds and animals, plants, etc. 293 illustrations. vii + 286pp.

20985-7 Paperbound $2.50

PETER PIPER'S PRACTICAL PRINCIPLES OF PLAIN & PERFECT PRONUNCIATION. Alliterative jingles and tongue-twisters of surprising charm, that made their first appearance in America about 1830. Republished in full with the spirited woodcut illustrations from this earliest American edition. 32pp. $4\frac{1}{2}$ x $6\frac{3}{8}$.

22560-7 Paperbound $1.00

SCIENCE EXPERIMENTS AND AMUSEMENTS FOR CHILDREN, Charles Vivian. 73 easy experiments, requiring only materials found at home or easily available, such as candles, coins, steel wool, etc.; illustrate basic phenomena like vacuum, simple chemical reaction, etc. All safe. Modern, well-planned. Formerly *Science Games for Children*. 102 photos, numerous drawings. 96pp. $6\frac{1}{8}$ x $9\frac{1}{4}$.

21856-2 Paperbound $1.25

AN INTRODUCTION TO CHESS MOVES AND TACTICS SIMPLY EXPLAINED, Leonard Barden. Informal intermediate introduction, quite strong in explaining reasons for moves. Covers basic material, tactics, important openings, traps, positional play in middle game, end game. Attempts to isolate patterns and recurrent configurations. Formerly *Chess*. 58 figures. 102pp. (USO) 21210-6 Paperbound $1.25

LASKER'S MANUAL OF CHESS, Dr. Emanuel Lasker. Lasker was not only one of the five great World Champions, he was also one of the ablest expositors, theorists, and analysts. In many ways, his Manual, permeated with his philosophy of battle, filled with keen insights, is one of the greatest works ever written on chess. Filled with analyzed games by the great players. A single-volume library that will profit almost any chess player, beginner or master. 308 diagrams. xli x 349pp.

20640-8 Paperbound $2.75

THE MASTER BOOK OF MATHEMATICAL RECREATIONS, Fred Schuh. In opinion of many the finest work ever prepared on mathematical puzzles, stunts, recreations; exhaustively thorough explanations of mathematics involved, analysis of effects, citation of puzzles and games. Mathematics involved is elementary. Translated by F. Göbel. 194 figures. xxiv + 430pp. 22134-2 Paperbound $3.00

MATHEMATICS, MAGIC AND MYSTERY, Martin Gardner. Puzzle editor for Scientific American explains mathematics behind various mystifying tricks: card tricks, stage "mind reading," coin and match tricks, counting out games, geometric dissections, etc. Probability sets, theory of numbers clearly explained. Also provides more than 400 tricks, guaranteed to work, that you can do. 135 illustrations. xii + 176pp.

20338-2 Paperbound $1.50

PLANETS, STARS AND GALAXIES: DESCRIPTIVE ASTRONOMY FOR BEGINNERS, A. E. Fanning. Comprehensive introductory survey of astronomy: the sun, solar system, stars, galaxies, universe, cosmology; up-to-date, including quasars, radio stars, etc. Preface by Prof. Donald Menzel. 24pp. of photographs. 189pp. 5¼ x 8¼.
21680-2 Paperbound $1.50

TEACH YOURSELF CALCULUS, P. Abbott. With a good background in algebra and trig, you can teach yourself calculus with this book. Simple, straightforward introduction to functions of all kinds, integration, differentiation, series, etc. "Students who are beginning to study calculus method will derive great help from this book." Faraday House Journal. 308pp. 20683-1 Clothbound $2.00

TEACH YOURSELF TRIGONOMETRY, P. Abbott. Geometrical foundations, indices and logarithms, ratios, angles, circular measure, etc. are presented in this sound, easy-to-use text. Excellent for the beginner or as a brush up, this text carries the student through the solution of triangles. 204pp. 20682-3 Clothbound $2.00

TEACH YOURSELF ANATOMY, David LeVay. Accurate, inclusive, profusely illustrated account of structure, skeleton, abdomen, muscles, nervous system, glands, brain, reproductive organs, evolution. "Quite the best and most readable account,' Medical Officer. 12 color plates. 164 figures. 311pp. 4¾ x 7.
21651-9 Clothbound $2.50

TEACH YOURSELF PHYSIOLOGY, David LeVay. Anatomical, biochemical bases; digestive, nervous, endocrine systems; metabolism; respiration; muscle; excretion; temperature control; reproduction. "Good elementary exposition," The Lancet. 6 color plates. 44 illustrations. 208pp. 4¼ x 7. 21658-6 Clothbound $2.50

THE FRIENDLY STARS, Martha Evans Martin. Classic has taught naked-eye observation of stars, planets to hundreds of thousands, still not surpassed for charm, lucidity, adequacy. Completely updated by Professor Donald H. Menzel, Harvard Observatory. 25 illustrations. 16 x 30 chart. x + 147pp. 21099-5 Paperbound $1.25

MUSIC OF THE SPHERES: THE MATERIAL UNIVERSE FROM ATOM TO QUASAR, SIMPLY EXPLAINED, Guy Murchie. Extremely broad, brilliantly written popular account begins with the solar system and reaches to dividing line between matter and nonmatter; latest understandings presented with exceptional clarity. Volume One: Planets, stars, galaxies, cosmology, geology, celestial mechanics, latest astronomical discoveries; Volume Two: Matter, atoms, waves, radiation, relativity, chemical action, heat, nuclear energy, quantum theory, music, light, color, probability, antimatter, antigravity, and similar topics. 319 figures. 1967 (second) edition. Total of xx + 644pp. 21809-0, 21810-4 Two volumes, Paperbound $5.00

OLD-TIME SCHOOLS AND SCHOOL BOOKS, Clifton Johnson. Illustrations and rhymes from early primers, abundant quotations from early textbooks, many anecdotes of school life enliven this study of elementary schools from Puritans to middle 19th century. Introduction by Carl Withers. 234 illustrations. xxxiii + 381pp.
21031-6 Paperbound $2.50

THE PHILOSOPHY OF THE UPANISHADS, Paul Deussen. Clear, detailed statement of upanishadic system of thought, generally considered among best available. History of these works, full exposition of system emergent from them, parallel concepts in the West. Translated by A. S. Geden. xiv + 429pp.
21616-0 Paperbound $3.00

LANGUAGE, TRUTH AND LOGIC, Alfred J. Ayer. Famous, remarkably clear introduction to the Vienna and Cambridge schools of Logical Positivism; function of philosophy, elimination of metaphysical thought, nature of analysis, similar topics. "Wish I had written it myself," Bertrand Russell. 2nd, 1946 edition. 160pp.
20010-8 Paperbound $1.35

THE GUIDE FOR THE PERPLEXED, Moses Maimonides. Great classic of medieval Judaism, major attempt to reconcile revealed religion (Pentateuch, commentaries) and Aristotelian philosophy. Enormously important in all Western thought. Unabridged Friedländer translation. 50-page introduction. lix + 414pp.
(USO) 20351-4 Paperbound $2.50

OCCULT AND SUPERNATURAL PHENOMENA, D. H. Rawcliffe. Full, serious study of the most persistent delusions of mankind: crystal gazing, mediumistic trance, stigmata, lycanthropy, fire walking, dowsing, telepathy, ghosts, ESP, etc., and their relation to common forms of abnormal psychology. Formerly *Illusions and Delusions of the Supernatural and the Occult.* iii + 551pp. 20503-7 Paperbound $3.50

THE EGYPTIAN BOOK OF THE DEAD: THE PAPYRUS OF ANI, E. A. Wallis Budge. Full hieroglyphic text, interlinear transliteration of sounds, word for word translation, then smooth, connected translation; Theban recension. Basic work in Ancient Egyptian civilization; now even more significant than ever for historical importance, dilation of consciousness, etc. clvi + 377pp. 6½ x 9¼.
21866-X Paperbound $3.95

PSYCHOLOGY OF MUSIC, Carl E. Seashore. Basic, thorough survey of everything known about psychology of music up to 1940's; essential reading for psychologists, musicologists. Physical acoustics; auditory apparatus; relationship of physical sound to perceived sound; role of the mind in sorting, altering, suppressing, creating sound sensations; musical learning, testing for ability, absolute pitch, other topics. Records of Caruso, Menuhin analyzed. 88 figures. xix + 408pp.
21851-1 Paperbound $2.75

THE I CHING (THE BOOK OF CHANGES), translated by James Legge. Complete translated text plus appendices by Confucius, of perhaps the most penetrating divination book ever compiled. Indispensable to all study of early Oriental civilizations. 3 plates. xxiii + 448pp. 21062-6 Paperbound $3.00

THE UPANISHADS, translated by Max Müller. Twelve classical upanishads: Chandogya, Kena, Aitareya, Kaushitaki, Isa, Katha, Mundaka, Taittiriyaka, Brhadaranyaka, Svetasvatara, Prasna, Maitriyana. 160-page introduction, analysis by Prof. Müller. Total of 826pp. 20398-0, 20399-9 Two volumes, Paperbound $5.00

MATHEMATICAL PUZZLES FOR BEGINNERS AND ENTHUSIASTS, Geoffrey Mott-Smith. 189 puzzles from easy to difficult—involving arithmetic, logic, algebra, properties of digits, probability, etc.—for enjoyment and mental stimulus. Explanation of mathematical principles behind the puzzles. 135 illustrations. viii + 248pp.
20198-8 Paperbound $1.75

PAPER FOLDING FOR BEGINNERS, William D. Murray and Francis J. Rigney. Easiest book on the market, clearest instructions on making interesting, beautiful origami. Sail boats, cups, roosters, frogs that move legs, bonbon boxes, standing birds, etc. 40 projects; more than 275 diagrams and photographs. 94pp.
20713-7 Paperbound $1.00

TRICKS AND GAMES ON THE POOL TABLE, Fred Herrmann. 79 tricks and games— some solitaires, some for two or more players, some competitive games—to entertain you between formal games. Mystifying shots and throws, unusual caroms, tricks involving such props as cork, coins, a hat, etc. Formerly *Fun on the Pool Table*. 77 figures. 95pp.
21814-7 Paperbound $1.00

HAND SHADOWS TO BE THROWN UPON THE WALL: A SERIES OF NOVEL AND AMUSING FIGURES FORMED BY THE HAND, Henry Bursill. Delightful picturebook from great-grandfather's day shows how to make 18 different hand shadows: a bird that flies, duck that quacks, dog that wags his tail, camel, goose, deer, boy, turtle, etc. Only book of its sort. vi + 33pp. 6½ x 9¼.
21779-5 Paperbound $1.00

WHITTLING AND WOODCARVING, E. J. Tangerman. 18th printing of best book on market. "If you can cut a potato you can carve" toys and puzzles, chains, chessmen, caricatures, masks, frames, woodcut blocks, surface patterns, much more. Information on tools, woods, techniques. Also goes into serious wood sculpture from Middle Ages to present, East and West. 464 photos, figures. x + 293pp.
20965-2 Paperbound $2.00

HISTORY OF PHILOSOPHY, Julián Marias. Possibly the clearest, most easily followed, best planned, most useful one-volume history of philosophy on the market; neither skimpy nor overfull. Full details on system of every major philosopher and dozens of less important thinkers from pre-Socratics up to Existentialism and later. Strong on many European figures usually omitted. Has gone through dozens of editions in Europe. 1966 edition, translated by Stanley Appelbaum and Clarence Strowbridge. xviii + 505pp.
21739-6 Paperbound $3.00

YOGA: A SCIENTIFIC EVALUATION, Kovoor T. Behanan. Scientific but non-technical study of physiological results of yoga exercises; done under auspices of Yale U. Relations to Indian thought, to psychoanalysis, etc. 16 photos. xxiii + 270pp.
20505-3 Paperbound $2.50

Prices subject to change without notice.
Available at your book dealer or write for free catalogue to Dept. GI, Dover Publications, Inc., 180 Varick St., N. Y., N. Y. 10014. Dover publishes more than 150 books each year on science, elementary and advanced mathematics, biology, music, art, literary history, social sciences and other areas.